THE LETTER BOX

Sgt. Glover's WWII Letters Home

THE LETTER BOX

Sgt. Glover's WWII Letters Home

by

Tom Caccioppoli Glover

CONTENTS

ACKNOWLEDGMENTS

Many thanks to the people who helped make this project a reality.

First, thanks to the Glover family "chain of ownership" of the letter box throughout the years: Louise and Roy, Rich and Erna, Joan, Rob and Terri, and thanks to my wife Jane, who has a keen eye for, and who values, family treasures. Each had their own reasons for keeping the box and its contents safe for seventy-plus years.

Thanks to Constance Renfrow, a gifted editor who provided encouragement throughout the process. Her guidance helped to improve the book immensely.

Thanks to those who helped with research and suggestions: Katie Glover, Lauren and James Glover, Joseph Glover, PhD, Rich "Butch" and Erna Glover, Rich Jr., "Coast Guard Bob," John Tobin, and Andy Lover. Thanks to: Rebecca Jefferson, George A. Smathers Libraries, University of Florida; Mr. Richard Goldstein, *The New York Times*; and Mr. Les Jensen, West Point Museum.

Finally, thanks to Dad, for taking the time to write the letters.

About the Cover Art

Credit goes to my very patient daughter Katie (who had the courage to volunteer and visit the remains of Camp Shanks with me in 2014).

About the Author

Tom Glover is the Managing Partner of Attain Management Resources, LLC, a management consulting firm. Tom's career has provided him the opportunity to travel around the world and visit many interesting places; best of all, it enabled him to meet fascinating people.

Tom's next book, tentatively titled "The Forger Farmer," is a novel inspired by real-life events that took place on Long Island during the late 19th century. It tells the story of a man who conspired against his own family, and of the ensuing legal case that was so sensational, it made headlines across America.

PREFACE

This book is a factual account of a young soldier's experiences during World War II. It is an accurate description of the challenges he and the world faced during the tail end of the greatest conflict of the twentieth century, and is told through the hundreds of letters Sergeant Glover sent home to his family from 1944 to 1946.

In 1944, a few months after D-Day, my father Robert "Bob" Glover enlisted in the United States Army on his eighteenth birthday,. As a child, my understanding of his experiences in World War II had largely been founded on real and fictional characters I'd seen in movies and on television. In general, my father was a quiet and thoughtful man, and like many of his military comrades, did not openly share much about his wartime experiences. On rare occasions, he would tell stories about his army buddies, Slim and Whitey, and when he did so, it was clear that his army experience had been more than just a job; it had been eye-opening and a coming of age for him.

There was sufficient evidence to support that theory. He had kept several cherished items from his military days: his army jacket hung proudly but quietly in a closet for years; the German Mauser pistol he'd purchased following V-E Day was safely stored and only displayed in public on special occasions; and his photographs of bombed European cities and the "displaced people," who struggled to return to their lands and a normal life, were kept secure in his closet. He had purchased several books about WWII history and military campaigns, which he placed on the family room table for all to see. Yet, despite these memorabilia from his army days, he seldom discussed or commented on the war, making it difficult for our family to get accurate insight into his own wartime experience.

My understanding of his participation in the war had been relatively simplistic: like millions of other men and women, he had sacrificed months and years of his youth and risked his life to serve his country. And, like many of his fellow soldiers, he asked and received little in return.

I'd assumed that my father's parents and siblings had been deeply affected when he'd entered the service. They'd known of the dangers enlisted men faced—newspaper articles and radio reports described daily the horrors of war. The early 1940s was a difficult time for the Glover family. The Great Depression had severely affected the rural farming community of Cutchogue, Long Island, where the family had lived for generations; as a result, they were forced to seek a better life in urban New York City. The effects of the subsequent economic downturn, combined with the war effort, demanded sacrifices from everyone, not just the Glover family. My grandparents' viewpoint was similar to that of most other Depression and WWII-era parents. They needed to provide food, clothing, shelter, and education for their children, while at the same time being patriotic and supporting the war effort—even if it meant knowing their son would be in danger. And my father's siblings asked the same questions as millions of other brothers and sisters of enlisted men and women; certainly for Bob's younger siblings Butch and Janet, the key question was: when would big brother Bob return home?

Bob's letters home are literally a "six feet off the ground" view of WWII, and are not a historian's sterile look in the rearview mirror. His story is told in his own words through hundreds of handwritten letters sent home to his family. This is a soldier's unique perspective on the war, on the issues that affected his morale, and on the activities to rebuild Europe during the "Army of the Occupation" period. This story is an opportunity to get an in-depth, detailed look at what it was really like for a patriotic, strong willed, young, American man to participate in the world's largest conflict. The grueling military training in places like Camp Croft, the dangers of the voyage to Europe, the challenges of dealing with prisoners of war and displaced persons, the living conditions before, during, and after the war were all representative of the experiences of many men during WWII.

Most of all, this is the story of one young man's efforts to stay connected to his family during a prolonged absence, and in the process, to completely rethink everything he had known and wanted to that point, and how he gained a better understanding of the things that really mattered in his life.

A BOX IS FOUND

My understanding of the relationship between my father and his family during World War II changed significantly, and was deepened, following the discovery of a regular gray cardboard box in a closet in my grandparents' upper Manhattan apartment. In August 1986, my grandparents were moving out of their home of many years, and it was then that the box was found; in it were found hundreds of letters written by their son, my father, to his family during WWII. Though it had almost been discarded by accident, the box was rescued by my dad's younger brother, Rich (aka "Butch") and placed in storage; then my mother, Joan, took over its care, storing it for many years in the closet next to my dad's army jacket. The box continued to change hands; my younger brother, Rob, rediscovered the box years later and stored it in his closet, before eventually offering it to me. Knowing that the box had been "in circulation" for many years, I decided it was now my turn and responsibility to store the box.

Over the years, Rob, his wife Terri, and our older brother Joe, had occasionally dipped into the box to read a letter or two. The letter box provided a game of sorts—one never knew what one would discover. Some letters contained old paper money, now useless; others revealed self-portraits sketched in the margins. Many talked about the living conditions in Germany. But mostly the letters were about wanting to come home.

Curiosity finally overcame my inertia, and I decided to approach the box in a more meaningful way. The letters were more than seventy years old, and I was concerned about the fragility of the paper and other contents of the box. First, I inventoried the letters and arranged them in chronological order. I was surprised to discover that my father—whose brevity was a well-known trait—had actually written more than two hundred letters in less than two years!

1

I felt I owed it to my father to read all the letters and to preserve them for posterity. After all, he and many other men and women had risked their lives to give me the freedom and ability to read these letters.

Upon initial inspection, it appeared that each envelope must have been opened very carefully, likely with an exceptionally sharp blade. The slits were perfectly made, as if a craftsman had made the cut. It was necessary to squeeze each envelope gently, in order to coax the opening to appear. I imagined that my grandfather Roy had taken great care to ease the envelope flap open with his ubiquitous pocketknife or my grandmother Louise (nee Macomber) had gracefully used her letter opener to reveal the contents. Either way, someone had taken great care to keep from damaging the documents.

The envelopes and the letters in the box survived mostly intact for seventy years, preserved since the end of WWII. However, the words were fading, so I decided to capture the contents and transcribe each letter for digital safekeeping. Pencil lead does not age well after seventy years, and pen and ink does not fare much better. As I typed each letter, I realized how tragic it was that we hadn't looked deeper into the box years earlier. Our family would have found that it contained a great story.

The letters tell the story of one young man, no different than millions of others, who traveled thousands of miles from home and risked his life to re-establish peace and stability in the world. They detail how my father's attempted to maintain closeness to his family through frequent communication, all while having the responsibilities of a soldier, thousands of miles away, during the most tumultuous time in modern history: World War II.

I wish I had taken the time to read the letters years ago. Doing so provided insight into my father and his family, and insight into a world war that I could have never gained through any formal school setting.

As I read through the letters, I heard my dad's voice, a man known for his simple and straightforward philosophy of life, whisper, "Better late than never."

∞∞ ∞∞ ∞∞

To best understand the content and the messages contained in the letters, it is important to understand Bob's writing style.

The majority of his letters were written to his mother, though others were written to close family members, and are often in a familial tone. Bob's somewhat staccato sentences were intentional; he took pride in his ability to write succinctly, and his words were chosen as he would have spoken them. The language used in the letters is often a continuous flow of thoughts, ideas, questions, and comments. This type of communication seems to be a Glover/Macomber family trait, handed down from generation to generation.

The letters in the book are as he wrote them. However, some of the greetings, salutations, opening phrases, and endings of the letters in this book have been intentionally omitted from the story to provide a sense of the continuity from letter to letter.

Unless indicated otherwise, the letters are written by: Robert Glover US Army Serial number 42161467. The vast majority of the envelopes are addressed solely to:

Mrs. Louise Glover
599 W 178 Street
New York 33, N.Y.

The letters almost always begin as *"Dear Mom"* or *"Dear Mom and family"* and almost always end with *"Love, Bob."*

An ellipsis (. . .) represents edited/omitted phrases, or sentences that contain repetitive ideas like "Well haven't got any

3

mail from you" or similar language. Commas and periods have been added in some places for clarity.

The day of the week Bob indicated on his letters is not always accurate; the reasons for this are explained in several of the letters.

Bob added single or double underlines when he felt that he had misspelled a word. This habit may have been a learned behavior from a former schoolteacher's corrections on his essays. In addition, he was often in a rush when writing the letters and usually had to return to his duties without the opportunity to reread what he had written. Most of the misspellings remain as written.

∞∞ ∞∞ ∞∞

Today, we take for granted the ability to send messages within seconds on a global scale. To say that intercontinental communication during the 1940s was different—especially during World War II—is an understatement.

The fastest way to send a letter in the 1940s was by airmail; in 1945, airmail routes often took ten days from Europe to the United States, although they sometimes took longer. This lengthy period of time often caused Bob to reply to a letter that had been written weeks, possibly even months earlier, so the chronology of comments may seem a little out of order.

Perhaps, it is also of interest to note that as I pulled the letters from their envelopes for what may have been the first time in almost seventy years, occasionally, a small piece of pipe tobacco would fall out with the papers. This particular legacy is most likely the remnants of one of my grandfather Roy's favorite pastimes.

THE GLOVER FAMILY, AN INTRODUCTION

Robert "Bob" Glover was born in 1926 to Roy and Louise Glover of Cutchogue, a rural farming town on the North Fork of Long Island. His father, Joseph LeRoy "Roy" Glover, was the son of a farmer, from whom he had inherited the ability to earn a living using his hands. The Glover family clan had lived on the North Fork for three hundred years, working as farmers, shipbuilders, and carpenters, and each generation had proudly performed their civic duties when their town or nation required it.

Roy was a great wit with an outgoing personality; he enjoyed good jokes and stories, and often indulged in a sip of whiskey and a parejo cigar while telling them. One of his favorites was to tell his grandchildren that he didn't know his exact age, claiming, "The building with the records burned down," or that "The Indians who raised me didn't know the year I was born." We knew his records weren't lost in a fire or to the fading memory of an imaginary Corchaug Native American tribe member; as Louise, his patient wife, confirmed his birthday was November 21, 1899.

Although born into a farming family, Roy decided at an early age that farming was not for him. He learned carpentry and earned a living working for the local highway department.

In his youth, Roy was evidently a bit of a handful for his parents, who were church-going Methodists and lived in a century-old log cabin. One story in particular provides insight into Roy's wild youth: Roy and a friend would often hop on an Indian-brand motorcycle and while riding, would shoot at varmints in the fields with a .22 caliber rifle. Roy's behavior subdued somewhat after he met and married Louise. Louise was a strong-willed woman who insisted that if Roy chose to continue his cigar smoking and whiskey drinking, then he must do so outside, in the barn. She continued to direct him "into the barn" even after they moved to their New York City apartment.

5

Bob's mother was born Louise Ursula Macomber in May, 1901 on East Eighty-first Street in New York. For the majority of her childhood, she and her family lived in Greenport, on the eastern end of Long Island, New York. From 1900 to the 1920s, the town of Greenport supported businesses related to fishing and sailing, and provided services for ships, crew members, tourists, and commercial and sport fishermen.

Through her mother's German ancestry, Louise proudly asserted that her family had ties to the famous German poet Schiller. Her family was unaware that their lineage on her father's side also could be traced to the voyage of the *Mayflower*.

Roy and Louise married in 1922, and explored the possibility of building a new home for their growing family. One of the options available was a novel method for the selection and payment for a new home. Beginning in 1908, The Sears, Roebuck and Co. offered consumers a choice of 447 homes for purchase through their mail-order catalog service. One had only to select the model from the catalog, and Sears would ship the pieces of the house by rail; then the buyer would be responsible for assembly and construction. Roy and Louise decided on a model from the catalog, and Roy put his carpentry skills to good use, constructing the house near the intersection of the Main Road (Rt. 25) and Cox Lane. This served as the Glover family home for many years, before they made the move to the city in the mid-1940s.

Roy and Louise had four surviving children: Ruth (nicknamed "Dolly") was the oldest, born in 1922; Bob, born in 1926; Janet, born in 1935; and Richard ("Rich" or "Butch") born in 1937. Another son, David, died at an early age of a childhood illness.

Cutchogue and the surrounding towns relied chiefly on agriculture for economic stability and tax revenue; therefore, the depression hit the community hard. The Glover family was no exception; local tax receipts declined, causing the town to cut costs. Unfortunately, this included the elimination of Roy's position. The family needed an income, and finding a new opportunity for employment on the North Fork was difficult at best.

In 1942 and 1943, Roy found work in the Brooklyn Navy Yard helping to build ships for the war. The 180-mile round trip commute from the east end of Long Island to Brooklyn was too far for Roy to consider commuting, so the family decided to leave Cutchogue and relocate to an apartment in upper Manhattan, a few city blocks from the George Washington Bridge.

Three of the children acclimated quickly to their new life in the city. Dolly, the oldest, continued her education and found employment in the financial industry. Janet and Butch were quickly enrolled in public elementary school.

Bob's transition was not as smooth. He had attended high school on the North Fork, but unfortunately, at the time the family moved, he had not gathered enough credits for graduation. Luckily, Bob was able to secure a job working with his father in the Brooklyn Navy Yard, which helped ease the family's financial situation.

Looking back, Bob and Roy's employment in the Navy Yard brought the Glover family full circle. Over three hundred years had elapsed since their ancestors had arrived in North America, but not much had changed in terms of the family's employment; the Glovers were continuing the family tradition of building ships in a shipyard.

∞∞ ∞∞ ∞∞

The Glover family was fiercely patriotic, but not blindly so. They had a sense of how World War II was affecting the "common people" in Europe. Louise took the position that "not all Germans" were evil, like Hitler. She explained that although there was good reason to fight the Nazis, there was great debate in the late 1930s and early 1940s about the United States getting too deeply involved in the war. A significant number of German immigrants to the United States had relatives still living in Germany; this was not unlike the situation during the Civil War, in which family members fought against each other. In their new home, Roy and Louise were reminded daily of the horrors of the Nazi regime. One of their neighbors offered a very real example of how Hitler's reign had affected several groups of citizens. The neighbor revealed the identification number the Nazis had tattooed on his arm and described how he had made his escape from early wartime Europe to come to New York.

Despite the uncertainty of war and their concern regarding the actions of the Nazi regime, it is no surprise that Roy and Louise were deeply proud of their son Bob when he registered for military service on his eighteenth birthday: July, 28th, 1944.

1944

PVT. GLOVER'S INDUCTION AND BOOT CAMP

As a teenager, Bob Glover was faced with several new challenges after being thrust from a small rural farm community into the big city of New York. Finding a meaningful job with sufficient pay posed unique challenges for the seventeen-year-old who did not have a high school diploma.

Bob was in competition with many men who probably had more experience, and so he used his common sense and quick wit to quickly land a job at the Brooklyn Navy Yard repairing and building ships for the war effort. These talents were the result of the work ethic he'd developed growing up in a blue-collar farming community; plus, his parents, Roy and Louise, were greatly influential to the development of Bob's positive attitude and behavior.

Bob was always interested in news, including local and world events. Though he did not have a college education, he understood the impact of major political, economic, and world events. He was insightful and often demonstrated a keen understanding of human nature and its strengths and weaknesses. For instance, if someone came to him to discuss a problem, he would listen intently and his reaction was often simply:

"There is no need to worry about ninety-seven percent of the issues we are faced with on a daily basis—these are the ones that are of little to no consequence in life. Identification of the ones that will be of significant consequence, the remaining three percent, and *doing something* about those issues will be of benefit."

He may have unintentionally been paraphrasing Mark Twain, who famously wrote: "I've had a lot of worries in my life, most of which never happened."

∞∞ ∞∞ ∞∞

9

At work in the Navy Yard, Bob overheard people from diverse backgrounds discussing their varied points of view on politics, sports, the economy, and the war. However, the war was the predominant topic of discussion. Everyone knew that soon Bob, too, would have to face entering military service. In 1944, Bob became one of the thousands of men who received a selective service notice. By the end of the war in 1945, fifty million men between the ages of eighteen and forty-five would register for the draft, and over ten million would be inducted into the military.

On his eighteenth birthday, July 28, 1944, Bob walked from his home on 178th Street to the Selective Service Local Board Office No.66 on 660 West 181st Street, where he completed the registration process. After waiting in line with many other eighteen-year-olds, Bob's height was recorded at 6' 0" and his weight registered at 160 pounds. His Selective Service card indicated that he had brown hair and brown eyes and a ruddy complexion. His race was recorded as white, and it was also noted that he had a scar on his left knee. The origin of the scar was of no military significance—it was the result of an accident with a cauliflower knife during harvest. His place of residence indicated the address he would write on hundreds of envelopes over the next two years: 599 West 178th Street, NYC.

Bob's registration brought with it mixed feelings for the Glover family. As has been mentioned before, they were fiercely patriotic and proud of the steps Bob had taken toward registering, but the family was also realistic. On a daily basis, radio stations and newspapers reported the number of US soldiers who were being injured, captured, and killed all over the world.

Despite these news reports, Roy was exceptionally proud of his son, telling his coworkers at the Navy Yard that his son joined the effort to fight the Germans, the Italians, and the Japanese.

Louise was also proud, but more reserved. She had relatives living in Germany and other parts of Nazi-occupied Europe and so was careful to point out that the aggression was not the people's fault, but the fault of the German politicians and the German military.

Following the news of the events of June 6th, D-Day, and Bob's registration on July 28th, the Glover family became increasingly aware of the gravity of the war; each day newspapers were reporting more and more shocking events. Beginning in early August, General Patton's 3rd Army encountered the Germans in France. In mid-August, several brutal battles resulted in the deaths of over ten thousand German soldiers, causing several German armies to surrender to the Allies at Normandy. In all, some fifty thousand soldiers of the German Army were taken prisoner, and by late August, Paris was liberated by the Allied troops. The United States Army and Allies moved from west to east, while the Russian army pushed the Germans from east to west, continuing their efforts to squeeze the German army between the two forces. These accomplishments were not without great cost to the Allies. On September 25th, it was announced that at Arnhem, six thousand Allied soldiers were taken prisoner by the Germans. A further one thousand soldiers had been killed.

∞∞∞ ∞∞∞ ∞∞∞

On October 1st, about two months after registering, Bob received his official induction notice, with instructions on where and when to report. On December 1st, he reported for duty, was inducted into the United States Army, and immediately transported to Fort Dix, New Jersey.

DECEMBER 1944, THE LETTERS BEGIN

CAMP DIX, FORT MEADE, AND CAMP CROFT

In 1939, Camp Dix, designated as a permanent Army post and renamed Fort Dix, became the reception and training center for thousands of United States Army inductees. Camp Dix served as many as ten divisions and several smaller units as they trained and staged in preparation for the battlefield.

Bob and his army buddies would spend the next few days here in their initial preparation for war. As he had promised his mother, Bob began writing letters as soon as it was practical to do so.

> *December 1*
> *Dear Mom,*
> *O.K. So far it is fine.*
> *I am at Dix it is about 80 miles from N.Y.*
> *It is just like Nassau Point.*
> *Fall Out*
> *They said for me to tell you not to write until we got where we are going.*
> *We will only be here a couple of days.*
> *Your Private,*
> *Son Bob*

Dec 2 Camp Dix

Dear Mom,

Well the whole company is restricted . . . most of us fell asleep in the theatre when some officer was giving a talk on fear and nobody wanted to listen to him anyhow so the CO got mad and restricted us all . . .

All we talk about is coming home . . . Me and a boy from 191st street are coming home in a taxi . . . ought to be home the 22nd of march if nothing happens . . . shot the mortar the other day + the knee mortar . . .

Dec 2 Sat night Camp Dix

. . . who said they don't give you clothes, that is the first thing they threw at us and enough: 5 shirts 2 woolen and 3 kaiki, 5pants, 5 pairs of underwear, 5 pr. socks, 2 pair heavy shoes + then your dress uniform. Pair leggings 3 hats + helmet and a million little things. They all fit fine. All my stuff is extra long.

This is a processing station. You only stay here 6 to 10 days then you get shipped to a training station.

I had a 'brain test' today . . . Monday I get two injections and my insurance and interview for assignment. I sleep in the upper berth. Don't write until I get someplace else. Don't send me nothing . . . if Dolly is going to get me a bracelet tell her to get the cheapest she can.

On Bob's second day in the Army, it is likely that he observed others as they fired mortars; it had to be an impressive experience for him and his new buddies.

During World War II, in addition to "dog tags," many soldiers wore Identification Bracelets, usually made of silver, stainless steel, copper, or aluminum. Name, rank, and serial

13

number were often listed, and it was common practice for a family member to have one made and sent to a soldier serving in the war.

Dec 5 Tuesday Camp Dix

Sunday I washed windows for a couple of hours . . . I got my shots . . . today I had K.P. in officers mess . . . I guess the army will be better than the navy . . . I hope to get in the engineers . . . they asked me to volunteer for the paratroops but I told them I had a weak knee . . . I seen "Meet Me in St Louis"! . . . my watch, pen and lights work fine

---

Dec. 6, 1944, Spartanburg, S.C.

Dear Butch,

Week after next we start to shoot our rifles but I wish I was home with you and Janet playing

I hope you get some nice presents for Christmas

Love

Bob

PS Drop me a line. I only got one letter from you.

KP or Kitchen Patrol was the term used for the activities performed in meal preparation and cleanup. This would be one of the many tasks Bob would learn as he went through basic training. Having grown up in a farm community, Bob was accustomed to getting his hands dirty, and he often welcomed the toughest, dirtiest assignments.

Dec 8 Camp Croft

. . . finally got on the move. It took 22 hr from Camp Dix on a troop train (NOW WRITE) . . . we went through Penn . . . + SC . . . The people live down here like pigs (NOW WRITE) . . . Arthur G. is in the same camp (NOW WRITE) . . . Monday we start our training for 17 weeks then we have a 10 day furlow plus traveling time (NOW WRITE) . . . Now you don't get anymore letters till you send me one . . . (NOW WRITE, oh yes, I am in the infantry . . . see you all in 12 weeks) . . .

Dec 9 Camp Croft

Well today we got on the ball first thing we got a G.I. haircut then we had some drill for about 6 hrs. We wore leggings.

Monday we start with our M-1 rifle + we learn to shoot anything from a rifle to a bazooka, rifle grenades, hand grenades, + everything else B.A.Rs+ carbines.

They claim to give you a better training than any Marine ever thought of getting.

I guess you know I'm in the infantry

Don't forget to write

You had better take some of my money home and buy all of you a Christmas present . . . now I think I will write to both Grandmothers . . . Oh yes you got that Red Cross card if anybody in the immediate family gets sick see them and I will get a furlough . . . so now I go to chow so good night . . . Darn good eats . . . (No mail yet . . .)

Dec 12 Tuesday 8:55 PM Camp Croft

Not much time to write + I am tired . . . yesterday 16 hrs of K.P. and today we run for a mile + ½ + then do exercises for the rest of the morning + in the afternoon we marched for about an hour then we learned how to take our rifle apart + put them together . . . after that we had two movies and a talk by Gen. Hester. After that we ate and I went to the P.X. . . . . and come back at 9:00 + washed socks +underwear

I am so tired and stiff I cant move . . . we have to shave every day

The mud is about 6 in. deep

Haven't got any mail yet

Please send me $5.00 in registered mail please no money order because it is to much trouble to cash it . . . write me . . . tell me all the news+ tell me what you heard from the Navy Yard. . . . Please write . . .

Dec 14, Thursday Camp Croft

Well you can write. Thank you "Doll" and thank for the candy. Don't send such a big box next time . . . sorry to hear that Uncle Emil is worse . . .

They give us one thing after another fast, land mines first aid, target tracing Military Discipline, health, + everything else all in one day oh yes I forgot map reading.

Weather they know it or not some of these things they tell us scare the hell out of me . . . i have been going all day from 6 AM to now 9:15 PM but I guess I will get used to that all really I don't mind it.

Sometimes now I catch myself walking around at attention.

I just got your letter the first one from you. I thought you had deserted me. I was scared. Glad to here from you write often

We get some issues every day. Today we got our steel helmets, Bayonets, pup tents + ammunition belts.

Sometimes I wonder if I will ever be able to stick somebody with my bayonet or shoot him with my rifle. I don't think I have the guts. But I guess they will put that in our minds.

Tell Butch and Janet I will be home in 17 weeks if nothing happens.

Oh yes we have two mail calls . . . I want to get a letter at each one

No use in saving the papers cause we can buy them at the post exchange

I got a G.I. haircut . . . when I get a chance I will get a picture taken . . . We have darn good eats.

After breakfast we run for about a mile +1/2

It is pretty near 10 o'clock so good night.

The continued reference to "darn good eats" was Bob's way of reassuring his mother that he was enjoying the food served. Louise knew that he was strictly a "meat and potatoes" type, with little deviation—unless it was time for dessert.

Dec 15 Friday Camp Croft

Well I have been hear a week and I cant find nothing wrong with it.

Today was a good day for mail 3 letters keep them coming

The boys all got a kick out of Butch's letter

Tell him the boys say to call it a rifle not a gun.

> *Today we had close order drill with our rifles+Gas mask drill. We have swell officers especially our captain. He calls me Clover. He is a little short guy name Hughs*
>
> *Today I was interviewed I got 119 in my I.Q. enough for Officers Candidate school but I don't believe I made a good enough impression*
>
> *I don't need anything. We got plenty of cigarettes and candy.*
>
> *Next weekend I can get a pass good only for 5 mile radius. I guess I will just stay in camp. Because anything you can do there you can do in camp cheaper. They even have 9 beer gardens . . . all our officers + non-coms are veterans . . .*

> *Dec, Saturday*
>
> *Well we left Ft. Meade and arrived here. All mail is censored now. I don't know what's up but we are moving fast. What I told Aunt Ruth came true . . . dont take this letter wrong I haven't left the US. Plenty of cigarettes here wish I could bring some home . . . there isn't much else I can write about but please write soon + often . . . if you don't here from me for a long time don't worry*

Bob's journey during his first few weeks in the Army was the longest he had traveled in his eighteen years. His longest trip prior to the Army was when he had traveled ninety miles from the east end of Long Island to New York City for 4-H club activities. Now, in less than two weeks, the Army transported him hundreds of miles from Manhattan, to Fort Dix in New Jersey, to Fort Meade in Maryland, to Camp Croft in South Carolina. Fort Meade was a training center during World War II and was the largest military facility Bob had seen to date. Approximately 3.5 million men were trained there between 1942 and 1946.

> *Dec 15 Sunday 8 AM*
>
> *Today I am room orderly and Fireman that is why I am up so early*
>
> *Most of the boys are still sleeping. Some day to be fireman. The only day we have off*
>
> *Yesterday we went through a gas attack + then we threw a couple of hand grenades. White Phospherase, schrapnel + ones with different color smoke + a mortar cocktail +you don't want to get near any of them + after that we had dry target tracing with our rifles*
>
> *At nights there are four of us that play cards*
>
> *You asked me what I wanted for Christmas . . . well all I want is a money belt you can take my money + buy that, get a cheap one + two pairs of brown woolen socks and a box of candy, thats all ("time drags on . . . a week is like a year")*

Every day, Bob learned more about life as a soldier. The terms "room orderly" and "fireman" were used to describe some of the basic duties a soldier performed under supervision.

Bob was learning about basic guns and much more dangerous weaponry, like white phosphorus (WP). A chemical that had been used in warfare as early as World War I, white phosphorous was considered to be as dangerous to the United States soldiers as it was to the enemy. When the material was packed in bombs, it needed to be stored in cool locations and, if possible, under water. One had to take precaution during handling to avoid cracking the bombs and accidentally releasing the material.

Despite the danger to its own soldiers, the US Army and Marines successfully used white phosphorous as an offensive weapon in battle against experienced German soldiers in World

War II. Shrapnel is simply the many pieces of metal debris resulting from exploding artillery shells or grenades.

Dec 15 Sunday

Well its Sunday morning and we got a half day off. All we have to do is clean the rifle, shave and about 1 million other things . . . I guess 2 weeks from today we will start home . . . Tell Butch and Janet I haven't forgot about the Ice Cream sodas . . . hope you got my watch ok . . . Friday night we start back to camp croft . . . well I have got $40 saved up and we are supposed to get paid again before we come home but I want to buy a lot of junk . . . can you get cigarettes in N.Y. . . . I think I will bring home a bunch of them anyway. . . . It is still dark and I am writing this in my tent by candle light . . . hope you can find me in the pictures . . . I am the guy standing in the back . . . + the other one I am the guy on the ground with the bayonet in me . . . tell Dolly to become Personal Mgr. so maybe she can hire a veteran after the war . . . All I think about now is my furlough . . .

The war looks good from down here

Well I guess I will close the sun is come up

Dec. Tuesday

Somewhere in S.C.

Dear Mom,

Well we are on maneuvers it isn't too bad . . . I think it is the 17th . . . you said you didn't get my watch . . . I sent it with that pen holder I sent you . . . tell Butch and Janet we will have more Ice Cream soda when I get home than they have ever seen . . . General Hester was out to see us yesterday +he says the war looks good, lets hope so . . . + don't forget next Saturday

---

Dec 19 Tuesday

Received 3 packages so far of candy and cookies

Received Bracelet which is to darn good it is the best one I've seen yet. Thank Dolly a million . . . also received the $5 . . . and Dolly's letter with $1 in it

. . . this started at 6 AM and just finished at 8:30PM.

This morning we went into a gas chamber with our masks.

Then we had flame throwers+ more hand grenades.

In the afternoon we had camouflage+ at night we had more about our M-1 rifles

Yesterday I complained about my knee+ they gave me pills it didn't hurt. I did it just to see what they would say.

Dec 20 Wednesday Camp Croft 7:00 PM

Thanks for the $5. I didn't need it . . .

About getting a transfer it would be all right but I wont want a discharge out of 240 in our Battalion 2 got discharges + both of them cried like babies when they got them

Anybody who tells you the marines are any better than the Infantry you can tell them they are crazy.

We don't get paid this month

This weekend we can get out of camp

My knee don't hurt but if it does or anything else I will drop out.

The guys are all O.K.

Well I got to wash my pack +overshoes+leggings+clean my rifle.

Dec 21 Thursday

. . . most of the day we had concealment from aircraft +then we had camoflaug besides our 1 mile run exercises we have off Sunday and Monday

We can go in a 200 mile radius a lot of good that will do . . . only thing we got 2 Sad Sacks in or platoon

Merry x mas . . . I'll be home next Xmas

Dec 22 Friday Camp Croft 9:30 PM

Had inspection again . . . everything O.K.

The Captain told us we are a replacement unit for Europe . . . if he knows . . . he says the war is going to last a long time yet . . .

Well we get out this weekend. But I think K.P. is rolling around Christmas. I got to go + fill out 2 laundry slips and shave and go to be(d).

See you in 15 weeks . . . tell Butch and Janet I be home pretty soon . . . Merry Xmas.

Bob, nine years older than his sister Janet and eleven years older than his brother Butch, played the classic "big brother" role to his younger siblings. From a young age and especially during the Great Depression years, Bob felt the need to help support his family economically, and he wanted to ensure that Butch and Janet were given opportunities that he had not had. He would not have wanted Butch and Janet to worry about him.

Dec 25 Christmas Camp Croft

Well it is 9:15 and I am still in bed. It don't seem like Christmas here

Yesterday I had 12 hrs of K.P. + then I went to Spartenburg. It don't seem to be no bigger than Greenport. Friday we had a 2 ½ mile hike.

Last night I went into the U.S.O. + they were singing Christmas Hymns + I felt pretty sad . . . I hope you all had a merry Christmas

Friday we has 2 more shots in the arm . . . I don't know what for

I get plenty of mail

There isn't nothing I can write about

Hope you are all well+fine only 15 more weeks + then I will be home.

Remember I used to talk about staying in the army after the war . . . well the day the war is over I'm starting home.

I hope it don't last much longer.

Week after next will be the toughest week all the time we will have to go to the range it is about three miles away.

Well I'll say goodby + a merry Christmas + a happier New Year.

Dec 27

Today we had a ten mile hike just a breeze. We just got through at 9:30PM. Last night we worked to 12.

Received your package with money belt socks and candy. Don't need anything else. There isn't nothing to write about.

New Year's Eve I am going to have guard duty

Had a good turkey Christmas

Three guys went over the hill so far . . . "good candy"

The term "over the hill" was common used to describe soldiers who left their post or responsibility without permission.

23

The more formal term used by the armed forces in these circumstances is "AWOL" or "absent without leave"

Dec 28 Camp Croft

It's exactly 9 o'clock just got thru G.I. party. That is when you scrub the barracks or anything else+ you scrub it till the wood is white.

This morning we had squad formation+ more about land mines and booby traps.

They keep you going as hard as they can all day + all night any body looks cross eyed at you, you want to knock there head off . . . i have to shave so will sign off . . .

P.S. a Sad Sack is a guy who isn't on the ball . . . Received $2 from Gram Glover

---

Dec 29 Camp Croft

I received a letter from you saying how cold it is in N.Y. Well I bet if you come down here you would probably freeze to death.

Today I had on long underwear, fatigue suit, field jacket, overcoat+ raincoat + I still was cold. . . . Sometimes I get so discussed I would like to run away but then you get back on the ball.

One of our sad sacks looks like Steve but shorter.

By the time you get this letter I will have probably got knocked down by a rifle kick but. They say it hasn't got but 15 lbs. pressure . . . We start the 1st January. A good way to start the New Year.

Dec. 31, 44 (in envelope postmarked Dec 31,1945)

Camp Croft

I got the paper signed by the adjutant of the company. I guess it is as good as a notary . . . you would think it would be warm down here but it feels like zero

About that picture I was going to send well I can only get them taking in town + it isn't worth going there. I was there last Saturday night + it stinks.

Tuesday we start on the range with our M-1 rifles

We get a half of day off tomorrow for New Years . . . I hope we all have a better year

They are starting to show us movies to make us want to fight.

Got another shot yesterday I don't know what for.

Mail must be speeding up the letter you sent Wednesday I got Saturday.

Immunizations were mandatory for all military personnel. Initially, Bob received shots for smallpox, typhoid, and tetanus, and later he received several booster shots during his time as a soldier. The Army was very aware of the potential danger of these diseases, especially in certain combat areas in Asian, African, and European combat zones.

1945

JANUARY 1945—CONTINUING TRAINING, PREPARING TO FIGHT

January 1 1945

Camp Croft

It is going to be a tough week so if you don't here from me don't worry. We got a range week all week we get up at 6 + wont get back till about 9. We eat out there also.

Went out with Arthur Sarno last night but had to be home at 11:00 we had a pretty good time.

Got your package and a letter from butch today. Thank him.

There isn't nothing to say except I'm scared of that rifle.

They cut (our) training down to 15 week + maybe only a 5 day furlough

Well its 9:40 + I got to shave and clean my rifle good.

So don't worry if you don't here from me for a couple of Days.

Good night,

Jan. 2, 1945

Well we got through early today I guess we walked about 3 miles out and back to the range. Today we fired at 200 yds + I got 45 out of 60. I was afraid of my rifle but no more, it kicks like a baby.

In the afternoon I was setting up target . . . its behind a big bucks

26

> *+ you ought to hear those bullets wiz over head*
>
> *I'm trying to get rid of my dandruff with olive oil.*
>
> *I got 8 dollars left + they say we get paid the eighth. If I get enough I will send some home . . . if anybody writes + tells you I didn't write to them tell them I don't have no time. I just about find time to write to you.*
>
> *It was below freezing again today.*

> *Jan 3, 1945*
>
> *Camp Croft*
>
> *No mail in two days you are all slipping . . . got paid today $37. I am sending $15 home if I ever get to the post office*
>
> *On the range today I got in practice . . . 171 out of 220 qualified for a sharp shooter. I just is tired as I could be + all the rest of the group*
>
> *I just write so you get mail.*

Beginning in the late nineteenth century, Marksmanship Qualification Badges were awarded to US Army soldiers once they met certain standards. During WWII, the Army provided three levels of awards for shooting ability. Ranked highest to lowest:

- Expert (26 target hits or better out of 30 as an example);
- Sharpshooter or First Class Gunner (21 hits out of 30);
- Marksman or Second Class Gunner (16 hits out of 30).

However, the Army did not consider these awards permanent, and soldiers were required to re-qualify on a periodic basis.

Given his rural upbringing and knowing his father's ability to shoot a rifle while riding on the back of a motorcycle, Bob would have been very confident in his shooting ability and very proud of his accomplishment and award—especially in his first attempt to qualify.

> *Jan 7, Wednesday*
>
> *Envelope sent by airmail 6 cents,*
>
> *Got your package + it will do fine.*
>
> *Hope the watch got there O.K.*
>
> *Haven't had no time to write + wont have for the next 2 weeks. I will write when I can if possible.*
>
> *I tell you what that Saturday we come back from maneuvers I think it is the 17th.*
>
> *I will call you up at Uncle Emil's.*
>
> *Well I have got to sign off.*
>
> *Don't expect no mail for 2 weeks + Don't worry.*

In some instances, the days and dates of the letters are inconsistent, possibly because Bob was in a rush to finish or because he began the letter one day and finished it on another.

> *Jan 8 Monday*
>
> *Camp Croft*
>
> *Well I haven't wrote for a couple of days because we are having night problems + Saturday I was out with Arthur and Slept all day yesterday . . . received a letter . . . from Gram Macomber*
>
> *They gave me another insurance form to send home.*
>
> *. . . nothing to write about . . . today we took up another rifle the carbine it shoots 15 shots just as fast as you can squeeze the*

> trigger
>
> But it isn't as good as the M.1 because it can't shoot as far + it don't do much damage

The National Service Life Insurance (NSLI) program was created in 1940 to provide insurance for WWII service personnel. Millions of NSLI policies were issued under a variety of permanent plans and also as renewable term insurance. During the war, Bob was diligent about purchasing the insurance policies, but when he realized that at the end of the war, there would be zero to little return on his investment, he began a policy of his own. His policy was to ignore life insurance salesmen.

Later in life, unless it was required by law—like car insurance—Bob did not believe in insurance policies. He fared better by investing his spare money in the stock market.

> Jan 13. Sat. Eve. 7:00 PM
>
> Had a pretty tough week that's why I didn't write much, had 2 night problems kept us up to 12 o'clock + yesterday we went on a 10 miles hike yesterday + put up our tents + stayed a little while + got back about 9:00 so by the time you clean your rifle + do the other things its pretty late.
>
> The bottle of nuts got here O.K . . .
>
> They say our next week will be the toughest week + after that we get easier training.
>
> When you get this letter I may be marching because Tuesday afternoon, we start + stay there overnight + come back Wednesday. So if I don't write next week don't worry . . . now I am going to the P.X. + get the biggest Ice Cream Soda you ever seen

Ice cream was considered a special treat in the late 1930s and early 1940s. When United States grocery stores began to sell ice cream in the 1930s, it became enormously popular throughout the country; by World War II, it had become such an American symbol, that Mussolini banned all ice cream in Italy due to its iconic status as an American treat. Ice cream boosted troop morale so much that in 1943, the United States military became the world's largest manufacturer of ice cream.

The US Army arranged to have ice cream at the front lines and the Navy built a floating ice cream parlor capable of producing 1,500 gallons an hour.

Jan 14, Sunday morn 8:30

Well it is still early + most of us just come back from chow + are now back in bed. Had a good breakfast 2 fried eggs, grapefruit, + corn flakes with coffee +toast.

I bought a pillow case + sent it to you, let me know if you get it. You will also get a book about the infantry.

Tell Butch and Janet that I am going to try + buy a polo shirt that says my brother is at Camp Croft S.C. . . . Ask daddy if he would like some cigarettes

Pretty lousey day foggy + chilly . . . at the end this we finish our 1st phase of our training

---

In his letters home, Bob was reflecting on the completion of the first part of his basic training. During World War II, Camp Croft served as the basic training center for most Army recruits from New York, Pennsylvania, and New England. Men arrived in groups of sixteen thousand, and began the standard thirteen-week basic training program in phases. Recruits used M-1 rifles, Browning Automatic Rifles, anti-tank rockets, and infantry mortars on training ranges in the southern part of the camp.

Soldiers were challenged on obstacle courses and trained to fight in chemical environments, which included the camp's gas chambers and gas obstacle course. They also completed amphibious warfare training, which utilized real explosives to simulate the effects of wartime situations.

Ever the big brother, Bob thought to buy his younger brother and sister shirts emblazoned with the Camp Croft insignia. These were considered excellent gifts for enlisted men to send home.

Jan 18 Camp Croft

From the War Department

Office of the Chaplain

35th Inf. Tng. Bn.

Addressed to Mrs. Louise Glover

Nothing was found in the box or in the envelope

Army chaplains were essentially clergy in uniform; their chief responsibilities included: praying, counseling, preaching, and conducting weddings, baptisms, and funerals. They provided comfort and advice to officers and enlisted men, usually regarding the subjects of homesickness, marriage, alcohol abuse, suicidal thoughts, and military problems.

During World War II, chaplains worked in hospitals, stockades, and on troop ships; on the front lines, chaplains cared for the wounded and administered the last rites. They had the responsibility of selecting burial sites, writing death reports, and sending letters of condolence to the families.

The chaplain at Camp Croft was responsible for reporting recent events—physical and emotional—to parents, and to advise parents how to respond to their children' s letters to increase their morale.

Louise may have kept this empty envelope as a reminder of the name and address of the chaplain, in the event that she needed to contact him.

Jan. 19, Friday night

Well we have finished our primary basic training + what a week this was.

Thursday was the beginning . . . in the morning we got up about 4:30 + hiked 3 miles to the carbine range + back then in the afternoon we went on a 15 mile hike + ended up in the woods some place about 9:30

Then we pitched tents + went to sleep . . . almost froze to death got up at 5:30 Wednesday + walked about 4 miles to another joint + practiced scouting all day + up till 11:00 + got in about 1:00 AM + got up at 5 Thursday+ went to the bazooka + grenade rifle range

The bazooka is a swell weapon you cant miss with it but I don't think much of the rifle grenade it kicks to darn much. Shot it 6 times + it knocked me down twice but the bazooka just goes swhosh +its gone

Today we had demolition + hand grenades

We set charges of T.N.T., C2 + starch + then we through (threw) real live grenades . . . was a 6 mile hike out+back

You ought to here the shrapnel . . . from the shrapnel from the grenades go by . . . well now you know why I didn't write

There is a company beer party tonight from 8:30 to 12 to celebrate our tough week maybe I will stroll over if I can get up enough energy

It rains every other day and freezes every other night so you can imagine what mud there is here

Now we officially get only 13 weeks training + 2 week maneuvers

Jan 20 Saturday 6:00

We suppose to have had this afternoon (off) but we got 24 hrs. of fire guard instead . . . all we do is lay around the barracks till there is a fire some place then they take us in trucks there.

Monday night we have guard duty . . . starting tomorrow we suppose to have an easy week mostly classes on B.A.R., Mortar + Machine guns.

Let me know if you got that pillow case?

Suppose to go to the show with Arthur this afternoon.

You asked me what kind of packages I like well those 5 cent candies are the best . . . tell Carl-Bunkle to stay out of the army as long as he can it may look glamorous but it is if I live through the training . . . I know I will live in combat because it couldn't be any tougher

Army life for Bob was becoming familiar and routine—a little like being a member of a club. On Long Island, Bob was a member of the 4-H Club, which he enjoyed both for the friends he made and for the medals and awards he won at the 4-H fairs. The Army was no different; Bob became interested in acquiring the paraphernalia of a United States soldier. Decorated pillow covers were one example. The practice of exchanging gifts of pillow covers to and from enlisted men began long before the Second World War. Typically, these were silk pillow covers with silk-screened designs. Most often, a soldier, sailor, or marine purchased these pillowcases as gifts and sent them home to his family. The popularity of pillowcases as gifts reached its height during the 1940s, when they began to be mass-produced and could often be bought at the camp store.

"Carl-Bunkle" was a nickname that Bob had given to his older sister Dolly's boyfriend. Bob was not overly fond of Carl and would often take verbal shots at him in public forums.

Jan 23 Tuesday

Well yesterday I had guard duty that means you walk for 2 hrs.

I was lucky and had the first watch from 7:30 till 9:30 then I came back went to bed + got up 5:30 + went on K.P. + just got off at 9:00P.M.

We are now studying the B.A.R. 30 caliber light machine gun+ bayonets

Well I have to shave now and get ready for tomorrow . . . when I get to Spartensburg again I will get the polo shirts.

Saturday

Well Thursday we fired the light machine gun + I got 80 out of 104 + yesterday we fired the B.A.R. at field targets + today we had more on the mortar + bayonet drills + got 2 teeth filled I thought he was killing me. Got 4 or 5 more to fill.

Received a package today. Thank you

Arthur left for maneuvers today.

Some of the Battalions are getting 14 days fourlough.

Good night.

The timing of Bob's draft notice could not have been better when it came to dental care. Bob had not received any significant dental care at home, so when his teeth were examined during basic training, the dentists found a complete project waiting for them.

A convenient coincidence, Bob had enlisted at virtually the same time the Army Dental Corps had recruited maximum support to treat the soldiers. In November 1944, the Dental Corps' active duty strength reached its highest level in history, with 15,292 officers. Each Army division typically had more than thirty dental officers responsible for the dental hygiene and care of the enlisted men. Personal dental care was limited in the 1940s, and the Army could not afford to invest in the development of a soldier, only to have that soldier unable to fight due to a cavity.

These were busy times for dental officers. During World War II, Bob's comrades in arms had a significant number of dental problems; from January 1942 to August 1945, the Army Dental Corps completed over sixteen million tooth extractions, sixty-nine million restorations, and over two million denture procedures.

In total, over eighteen thousand dentists served during World War II.

Jan 27 Saturday Eve.

. . . we had a pretty easy week. . . we have finished 7 weeks it seems to go pretty fast . . . We had some more training on the B.A.R. + Machine gun . . . next week we fire the B.A.R. them things are some piece of work. The week after we fire the machine gun

I think of so many things to write when I am marching + in class or in the field but when I go to write I forget them . . . feel ok only thing very tired. The watch is beginning to lose a lot of time now + I got the lighter yet + this is the pen writing

---

Bob was impressed with the Browning Automatic Rifle, or the BAR as it became known; he had never seen such a powerful weapon. The BAR was an automatic weapon used in World War I and World War II. At the start of WWII, most infantries used two- to three-man teams to fire one weapon, as the BAR required assistants to carry and load the massive 30 caliber bullets contained in the magazines. This strategy had serious offensive limitations; it was commonly believed that the average combat lifespan of a WWII BAR gunner was only thirty minutes. The enemy would simply wait for the BAR magazine to empty, then would open fire as the gunners were focused on reloading their weapon.

The Army believed the solution was to use two teams; the first team would fire their BAR until it ran out of ammunition, when the second team would commence firing their BAR, allowing team one the freedom to reload. Still, it was tricky business for even the most experienced soldier.

During WWII, the BAR was used extensively in Europe by the Army and in the Pacific by the Navy, though the debate continues as to the effectiveness and reliability of the weapon.

It appears that Bob's ability to concentrate and focus on the matter at hand became challenging during this period of time. His letters repeat many subjects and sentences, which may have been a result of exhaustion, stress, and sleep deprivation. It was becoming evident that the stress of boot camp was taking its toll.

Despite the challenges, Bob persevered, and during this time, he developed the ability to fall asleep anywhere and at any time. This skill was put to good use during his years in the Army, and would also be valuable later in life, as his career would involve long hours of the day and night.

Jan 28 Sunday Eve

. . . Arthur came over last night + we went to Spartenburg . . . I went to the store to get some polo shirts but they were closed

Oh yes maybe I forgot to tell you last week I got a tooth pulled + got to have 6 filled + I got vaccinated for yellow fever

---

Jan 29th Monday

. . . we had an easy day today got off 5:30

Had some Hand to Hand Combat + machine gun.

Quite a few of the boys in the platoon are joining the paratroops. They are all gone crazy I guess but I guess they are so worked up they just don't care.

Now I am lying on my bunk eating peanut brittle + smoking. This is the life. We get a nice lb. box for 35 cents.

It hasn't rained here in about 5 days I guess that is a record for S. C . . . ask daddy how they are coming on the <u>CVB 42</u>

Prior to his induction into the Army, Bob knew his father had worked on, or would eventually work on, many of the famous warships at the Brooklyn Navy Yard.

The USS *Franklin D. Roosevelt* (CVB/CVA/CV-42) was the second of three *Midway* class aircraft carriers. *Roosevelt* spent most of her active deployed career operating in the Mediterranean Sea. The ship was constructed at the New York Naval Shipyard and christened the *Coral Sea* at the 29 April 1945 launch. On 8 May 1945, President Harry S. Truman approved the Secretary of the Navy's recommendation to rename the ship the *Franklin D. Roosevelt* in honor of the late president; she was the first aircraft carrier to be named for an American statesman.

Jan 30 Tuesday

Today we had 4 more hours on the B.A. R. + took up the 60 MM Mortar for 4 hrs.

Hope everything is alright on the home front. I can say that now because I am now considered a veteran.

I've got the future all figured out according to the G.I. Bill of rights you can go to school . . . for every day you were in the

> *army 1 day to any School, so I will go to a good sheet metal school for a while + you also get paid same as you were getting in the army . . . I will sign off because I have to pack a full field pack + go to the P.X.*
>
> *How is Carl making out?*

Bob may have gotten a little ahead of himself when he claimed he was considered a veteran. By the Code of Federal Regulations, one was considered a World War II veteran if you were in active service during the World War II period, and if no longer in active service, you were separated from that service under conditions other than dishonorable after at least ninety days of active service.

Stated simply, each soldier that was on active duty for at least ninety days and honorably discharged was qualified as a veteran. Combat experience was not required.

The GI Bill was signed into law in 1944 and provided college, high school, or vocational education for World War II veterans. It also provided one year of unemployment insurance, and loans for homes, businesses, and farms.

The Servicemen's Readjustment Act of 1944, better known as the GI Bill of Rights, was a hotly debated issue in Congress during the war. Many politicians thought it would be too expensive for the country to bear following the war. Others saw it as the most significant piece of legislation ever produced by the federal government. The bill offered benefits to WWII veterans, which was in stark contrast to the experience of returning WWI veterans. Following the end of WWI, veterans were sent home with a train ticket and sixty dollars. Many veterans were upset because they were not paid the wartime bonuses they had been promised; eventually, irate veterans marched on Washington, DC much to the embarrassment of politicians. The situation became increasingly ugly when US troops were called in to clear the veterans out of the capital.

The president and congress did not wish to repeat this situation; therefore, they passed the GI Bill supporting education and training, loan guarantees for homes, farms, or businesses, and unemployment pay.

The GI Bill resulted in a hugely successful program; prior to World War II, most soldiers could not afford a college education or to purchase a home. The bill changed much of that, and in 1947, veterans accounted for forty-nine percent of college admissions. By 1956 almost half of the sixteen million World War II Veterans had participated in an education or training program under the GI Bill.

At this point, Bob had successfully completed sixty days of wartime service. According to the regulations, he needed another thirty days to fully qualify for the benefits included in the bill. But he did not need to worry; his time served would more than qualify him.

FEBRUARY 1945—CAMP CROFT

Feb 1, Thursday

. . . we have been having it easy the last couple of days mostly classes.

Tomorrow we will have a tough day we fire the B.A.R. on the range

I just drop you a line to let you I am O.K. . . . there really isn't anything to write about

Feb 4 Sunday

Arthur came back from manoevers last night + we went to town

Well there is only a month before I will be home

Has daddy got an old pair of Brown shoes with a little shine on them? If he has I would like to have them to wear home. Don't think I'm too much of a bother because I am just trying to get set to come home . . . think I will shoot some pool this afternoon . . . and it's pretty near time to eat

Feb 4 Sunday 12 Noon

Last night went to Spartenburg with Arthur + had our pictures taken. These that I am sending cost $.50 apiece. After we got them taken he didn't want any.

Just had mail call + received your box of candy looks good.

Well to get back to the pictures they aren't much but they will have to do because the(y) want about $8 for a good one.

About the polo shirts I went in + the(y) wanted $9 a piece so I told them off.

I got you a cheap pin + a handkerchief + dolly+Janet a

hankerchief+Butch a banner. Tell Daddy I will try + find him something.

They try to rob the soldier in Spartenburg

Next week I am going to buy dolly a head piece.

Feb 5 Monday

Had an easy day It rained most of the day + we had inspections, talks, movies +Physical Training.

We are mostly having review now in one more month we will start our maneuvers

One guy fooling around with his rifle shot his big toe off.

I don't believe I will send any money home because now I have nights off+ I get more time to spend it+ I figure I might as well spend it now.

You asked about candy we get it for 4 cents but you cant get any chocolate

If I ever get to it I am going to send my watch home, it loses to much time . . . maybe we can get it fixed . . . if we cant we'll just have to throw it away

Bob liked watches, and well before Swatch watches became popular, he considered watches to be "semi-disposable," especially if they didn't work properly. This was in stark contrast to his father and grandfather, who were proud of the fact they had each used the same pocket watch for many years.

During World War II the use of a watch was considered necessary for ground and naval officers, aviators, and others with command or technical responsibilities. Official service watches were available, but many enlisted men either bought their own wristwatch or added a distinctive band to their military watch.

Similar to pillows, a watch was another keepsake of the WWII era, and many soldiers wanted them. In Europe during WWII, watches took on more than their intrinsic value and were considered tradable commodities.

Feb 7 Wednesday

I don't know, last year you know I was sick every other week, well now I stand in the rain all day + freezing + I don't even get a sniffel

Tell dad not to worry about me doing anything I don't have to.

Today we had some bayonet Drill . . . I guess that is about the wickedest weapon there is.

Feb 7 Wednesday

. . . today we fired the L.M.G. Light Machine gun got 90 out of 104 . . . fires just as fast as you can think.

You pull the trigger + let it go as fast as you can + it fires about 10 rounds . . . got a letter from Gram Glover today. She says a lot of boys have gone in the Army.

After you see these weapons you aren't afraid to fight.

Good night

Feb 11 Sunday

Received your Valintine today.

For three days now we have had nice weather we can go around in your shirt . . . Ma would you look around there+ see how much an O.D. Blouse is. You know the Jacket they call it a blouse.

This afternoon we are going to the Field House + shoot pool, getting pretty fair.

Why don't daddy get on Days, would be a heck of a lot better.

Was playing baseball this morning.

March 3rd we go on maneuvers for 2 weeks + come back here for a week then we get our fourlough.

Well its 1 o'clock so I guess we are going to shoot pool.

Feb 13 Tuesday

. . . it was raining cats and dogs but it turned out to be a beautiful day.

Now we are learning tactics. That is how to maneuver to take a hill + what each man should do.

It's hard running all over S.C. But it's a lot of fun.

We work like one Platoon holds a position+ another Platoon attacks + the(y) both fire blanks at each other.

We are all planning on our fourlough they say they are going to take us to N.Y. by troop train because most of the boys come from around there

---

Feb 14 Wednesday

No mail in a couple of days.

Today we fire another type of machine gun it has 2 legs in front + it rest up against your shoulder.

Today it must have been around 70 degrees with a bright sun.

Everyday we plan more+ more on coming home.

Well I got to get up early because I got table waiters.

"Table waiter" was the term used for soldiers who attended to the Army's needs during meals in the mess hall. They prepared the tables, ensured that everything was clean and orderly, and cleaned up after the meal.

Feb 15 Friday

. . . today I died again at the dentist but I am finally finished. I hope. Some Capt. From 207st N.Y. said I had good teeth.

You can send the bag now if you will.

Sometimes I feel everything is against me + then I don't give a darn what happen. I guess that is the way they want you to feel.

I am glad I only have 5 more weeks of this + then maybe I will get a rest.

Maybe I shouldn't write this but that is the way I feel now.

Tell Butch to write or I wont come home +tell Janet to stop making fun of him

Well I guess I will sign off because the kitchen needs to be G.I. + I'm on K.P.

Feb 17 Sunday

. . . we were restricted this weekend but the boys are still happy singing+ joking.

Got K.P. tomorrow

Could you get that package here next week sometime so I will have something to eat on maneuvers + I would like some candles. You see we put one of them under our steel helmet + its like a stove.

Another battalion went home on fourlough today. Wont be long before I am home it will be around Easter.

We call our platoon the Brush masters because that was the name of the Division our seargent was in the Pacific. . . .

Bob was attempting to be creative with the use of his helmet, likely at the urging of more experienced soldiers who had fooled him into thinking his helmet was a good tool for cooking food in the field. In reality, this practice was strongly discouraged by the US Army.

More than twenty-two million M-1 helmets were manufactured during World War II, and were issued to soldiers during basic training. The M-1, designed as a "one size fits all" helmet, came in two parts: the steel shell and a liner. The shell could not be worn alone, but the liner could be.

Necessity on the battlefield became the mother of invention, and soldiers used the helmet shell in many creative ways; for example, as a shovel, a washbasin, a bucket, and a seat. The shell was occasionally used as a pot, but the heat, unfortunately, made the alloy brittle, rendering the pot likely unsafe for cooking.

Feb 19 Tuesday

. . . yesterday I had K.P. + signed our fourlough papers.

It only cost about $1.50 for fare when I get through . . . will pay my way home but get most of it back after.

Got a letter from you where you are worrying about what is going to do after my fourlough. Don't worry I took care of myself for a while now + I guess I can make it the rest of the way. If you are going to worry about it you make me feel bad. There is a heck of a bunch of guys in this country + maybe I'll be lucky . . . if not + I have to go across, 9 out of 10 come back.

But please don't worry.

According to the National World War II Museum, there were approximately eight million soldiers serving in the United

States Army during 1944–1945. This number does not include other branches of the military.

By the end of the war, 407,000 US soldiers had been killed and 671,000 were wounded. So if we calculate the numbers and use Bob's terminology, nineteen out of twenty soldiers came back. The odds of coming back, in reality, were better than Bob thought.

Feb 21 Wednesday

Postmarked Feb 23, 11:30 AM, Cutchogue, N.Y.

Addressed to Miss Janet Glover

Dear Janet

I think you have a birthday some time this week but I can not remember what day so I am writing you this letter hopeing you will received it somewhere near the day + I thought you could do what you like with the money. I never did see so much snow all the time. I hope someone will come in and mail this letter for me.

Write to me some time and let us know how your Father is as we are very anxious to know how he is feeling. I received the little pictures of you and Dicky + think they are nice.

Sunday Frank stopped in and I let him look at the pictures and he laughed. He thought they were great.

Give my best love to all and write when you have time.

Gram Glover

Bob's younger sister Janet turned ten years old in 1945 and received a birthday letter from her grandmother, who at the age of seventy-one was still living on the farm in Cutchogue with her husband, Charles. Cutchogue, in the middle of winter 1945, was a very quiet place with few visitors, and they likely had no phone service in their log cabin.

Feb 27 Tuesday

I only got till tomorrow to mail the package if I don't send home war trophies after the first.

I cant seem to write a letter anymore.

Carl must be having a rough time. I guess he will make out alright you couldn't get it much softer than the Air Corp.

I seem to be getting madder at the Krauts. I wish something would happen so I could write something.

The boys in the line company are going to start training the first of the month

Hope I can stick where I am or get that code clerk. I wouldn't have any trouble with the machine.

Bob's comment about getting angry "at the Krauts" was fueled by the effects of his basic training and the ongoing news reports on the European conflict. By February 27, the terrible results of the war were apparent to Bob and the world. The German Army was being squeezed in the east by the Russian Army and in the west by the Allies, and the resulting death toll was staggering. The Germans lost eighty-two thousand men, slightly more than the seventy-seven thousand casualties suffered by the American Army. Less than a year after D-Day, the US death and casualty toll was much higher than predicted.

Bob's comments continue to reflect his dislike for Carl, and he insinuates that Carl must be having a difficult time, even in an "easy" and "soft" assignment like the Air Corp. These might seem as gentle pokes in writing, but when taken as a whole, Bob's repeated comments demonstrate that he did not find Carl an acceptable suitor for his sister.

MARCH/APRIL 1945—THE LETTERS CEASE

No letters dated March or April 1945 were found in the box. There are several possible reasons for this dearth of correspondence.

It is possible that Bob wrote several letters during this period of time, but they were censored as part of the V-mail system. V-mail, developed by Eastman Kodak, was a way for soldiers overseas to communicate with friends and family back home, allowing for faster, less expensive correspondence compared with airmail. V-Mail was considered a more secure method of communication; each letter was censored before it was transferred to microfilm. When V-Mail letters arrived at a central location, the negatives were blown up to full size and printed. The USPS saved thousands of tons of shipping space by fitting the equivalent of thirty-seven-mailbags worth of letters into just one.

A more likely scenario is that Bob was unable to write any letters, as he was busy traveling to Europe and could not send any communications. By the time Bob arrived in Europe in March 1945, he was preoccupied with performing the tasks of a soldier of the United States Army in the 106th Infantry Division (ID). It is likely he was too busy to write, as his arrival took place a few short months following the Battle of the Bulge.

THE 106TH INFANTRY DIVISION AND THE BATTLE OF THE BULGE. THE "LAST DIVISION"

The 106th ID was the final US ID of sixty-six divisions activated during the war. The 106th ID was split into two groups in late 1944; the first group included Bob's unit and was sent to basic training facilities in the United States.

The second group consisted of soldiers with limited training and no experience in actual fighting. This group departed for Europe from Boston Harbor on November 10, 1944.

The initial European-bound group landed in England for a short period of additional training and then crossed the English Channel, landing at LeHavre, France. They immediately traveled to the area of St. Vith in Belgium to fight the German Army in a snowy, hilly area known as the Schnee Eifel.

In December 1944, Allied soldiers in Schnee Eifel found themselves in a very difficult position against the Germans, especially the US 2nd ID, which had been involved in intense fighting with the Germans for weeks. The American military commanders decided the men of the 2nd Infantry needed a break from fighting and reassigned them to another area, with orders for the 106th ID to replace them. The newly minted soldiers from the 106th ID did not have much of a chance against the battle-hardened Germany Army.

Starting in the early morning of December 16th, the German Army, with eight thousand pieces of artillery, began pounding the US soldiers for three full days, cutting off two regiments. By the 19th, the outlook for the 106th ID was dismal. Their ammunition exhausted, the US commanders decided to surrender to the Germans rather than risk losing all their men. The 106th ID had been actively fighting in Europe for a total of five days.

The Germans took over seven thousand prisoners that day, in one of the largest mass surrenders in American military history. The men were divided into groups and sent to several POW camps. Only a few lucky soldiers were able to elude capture.

This event became known as the Battle of the Bulge.

Meanwhile, as the 7th Army was busy rescuing the soldiers from the 106th ID who had been taken prisoner, members of the first group of the 106th ID, including Bob, were preparing to make their way to Europe.

∞∞ ∞∞ ∞∞

Heading north by troop train in mid-March, Bob and his comrades from basic training left South Carolina knowing little to nothing about the fate of the members of the 106th ID who were captured during the Battle of the Bulge. The train stopped at Fort Meade for six days and again headed north arriving at 6 p.m. at Camp Shanks, a few miles north of Manhattan on the west bank of the Hudson River.

Camp Shanks, a US Army facility, was designed to provide the point of embarkation for troops during World War II. It was nicknamed "Last Stop USA" and processed over one million service personnel, including the majority of soldiers who landed in Europe during the D-Day invasion. Later, in 1945 the camp became a prisoner of war facility and housed both German and Italian POWs.

At Camp Shanks, Bob's family was only ten miles south, straight down the Hudson River. A few days later, the unit headed out again by train to 34th Street in Manhattan—again only a 30 minute train ride from his parents' home—then on to Staten Island by ferry. Their objective was to board the USS *Marine Devil*, a troop transport ship bound for England.

When they reached the ship, Bob and his army buddies waited on the pier for their names to be called. He climbed up the gangplank and boarded the military transport ship, where they were told they would bunk for an unknown period of time. Two weeks later, the USS *Marine Devil*, along with a large convoy of Destroyer Escort boats, sailed for Europe on April 15th. Their initial port was Weymouth, England, where the ship moored for a single night; then they sailed again, this time crossing the English Channel for the city port of LeHavre, France.

It was a dangerous journey for any ship to sail through the Channel. German U-boats had successfully sunk several Allied vessels. Bob later commented in his letters that he was never so scared as when the ship fought off several enemy submarines during their journey across the Channel.

Safely reaching LeHavre, Bob's first observation was that this would be the first of several "wrecked cities" they would see in their travels. Following one day in port, the men boarded a train and rode in a boxcar for two days and nights in the frigid weather. The unit was informed that they were going immediately into combat to fight the German Army in southern Germany. After a series of stops and starts on the train, Bob's intuition told him that plans had changed, and as he predicted, the unit got off the train in München Gladback (outside of Cologne, Germany) where they rested for a week.

They were then ordered to travel by truck to Lindel where the 106th ID was assigned to the 15th Army. The soldiers enjoyed a rare opportunity to shower—to their surprise, in a coalmine! They rested for two more days in Lindel, and then traveled to the city of Reich to spend the night. The unit's destinations frequently changed.

The unit's final stop was the town of Wickratherberg in the Rhine Valley; in his letters, Bob anglicized the name of the town as "Whitcraft." Here the unit was assigned the task of guarding German prisoners of war.

Bob and his buddies could not have known the reasons for the constant changes in for the unit. In reality, the end of the war was not far away.

On April 27th, the German 12th Army made a last-minute effort to protect Berlin. The Soviet Army, however, rapidly defeated them and forced their way into the city. On April 30, Adolf Hitler gave a final speech to his staff, married his mistress Eva Braun, poisoned his dog, and along with his new wife, committed suicide.

On May 1st, German propaganda minister Joseph Goebbels, also seeing the end was near, murdered his wife and six children, and then committed suicide. On that same day, what was left of the German military in Berlin formally and unconditionally surrendered to the Soviet and Western Allied military commanders.

∞∞ ∞∞ ∞∞

In April, the two groups from the 106th ID, including the former POWs, formally rejoined, and the 106th ID was once again reconstituted at Rennes in France. On April 25th, the reunited soldiers headed for Germany.

During the next few months, the primary responsibility of the 106th ID was to guard and process over one million German Prisoners of War who were being held in several POW camps. The 106th ID was specifically responsible for providing the POWs with basic necessities, including shelter, food, and transportation. The POW camps were often nothing more than wire-enclosed fields, where the POWs slept under canvas canopies.

The POW camp system under management of the 106th ID was divided into three major POW groups designated as Red, Green, and White. The Red area was commanded by Colonel H. J. Vander Heide, 3rd Infantry Regiment, and had three major POW camps under his control: Buderich, Rheinberg, and Wickratherberg. Bob and his unit were responsible for guarding the Wickratherberg camp.

Processing the POWs required a huge amount of time and detail. As many as nine thousand POWs were processed per day, and by July 10, 1945, the 106th ID left the camps, having turned over the last of the POWs to the French 10th Infantry.

MAY 1945—THE LETTERS CONTINUE

May 3 Somewhere in germany,

Well Folks I got as Far as Germany. I am feeling fine. 7 other fellows and I are living in a German Doctor's House. It is a beautiful house. Those guys over here had everything. I don't know what they want to start a war for.

I sent a banner from Ft. Meade hope you got it.

Yesterday we got (?) our rations for a week. You get 7 packs of cigarettes, 6 bars of candy 2 packs of gum+ what toilet articles you need+ a can of orange juice.

HOPE YOU CAN READ THIS

May 5 Somewhere in Germany,

Well Mom we are now living in a school house in Germany

I couldn't write about the boat ride in my other letters but we had a couple of weeks of rest + plenty of entertainment + good eats

When I get a chance I will send him the money for the insurance. I got 550 mark $55 + a month's pay coming.

I am not in combat. Just loafing around

Hope everybody is O.K. I am feeling better than ever.

This letter from Bob was a V-Mail letter, and indicates of the challenges of prompt mail delivery. The envelope is postmarked May 3, and Louise's handwriting on the envelope notes, "Received June 1 1945"—almost a full month after Bob wrote it.

Bob discovered months later that by May 8th, V-E Day, the 106th ID had experienced sixty-three days of combat, suffered 417 killed in action, 1,278 wounded in action, and fifty-three soldiers died of their wounds. 6,697 personnel were taken prisoner, and of that total, 6,500 POWs were eventually released to American military control at war's end. The remainder of the men were listed as missing in action.

> *May 12, Somewhere in Germany*
>
> *I hope this letter finds you in the best of health . . . I am feeling fine.*
>
> *The last couple of days it has been very hot over here pretty near sweating to death.*
>
> *Haven't got any mail yet because we have been moving around quite a bit*
>
> *I guess you had a big time in New York when you heard the war was over . . . how about some candy or peanuts + a rubber ball about the size of a Baseball*
>
> *P.S. Do not forget the candy*

Mail continued to be reviewed by the censors. "Passed by US Army Examiner 50006" was stamped on the front of the envelope.

> *May 14, 1945*
>
> *Somewhere in Germany*
>
> *Well here I am trying to write another letter. Hope all of you are O.K.*
>
> *Tell Butch that I have named my rifle after him.*
>
> *There are some rumors that we might get our mail in a couple of days + I hope I get a big stack.*

We got some free Hershey chocolates + cigarettes the other day.

Well to this point system of getting discharged. I only got about 9 + you have 85 to get discharged. So I figured out that it would take about 6 years over here or 12 years in the U.S. but they will probably reduce that after Japan.

I have seen quite a few cities + most of them are flat maybe it will take these guys a few years to build it up before they start another war.

I guess us guys who got here when we did got a big break.

I am still with about 10 guys from Camp Croft.

I hope you had a nice mothers day.

Germany, May 20, 1945

Dear Butch,

Got your V-mail letter today + was glad to hear from you.

Hope you are OK + so are the rest.

Well butch I been over here over a month now + I can find a NAZI they all say they aren't.

It is taking about 18 days for your mail to get here.

Well tomorrow I will have been in the army 6 months.

I'll bet I look at the pictures I've got 10 times a day I wonder if you would send some more.

How did my pictures come out I had taken for mom?

In May 1945, the War Department announced a point system for the discharge of soldiers stationed in Europe. Points were awarded for the amount of time served and additional points were granted for months of overseas service. Battle stars earned additional points, and soldiers who had children were given even more points. Once a soldier reached the required eighty-five points, they qualified to return to the United States as soon as transport was available.

May 23 Wednesday Whitcraft Germany,

Dear Mom + Dad,

Well now I can tell you the story of my travels, we as you know went to Ft. Meade and stayed 6 days. Saturday afternoon we left and got to Camp Shanks about 6 o'clock. I thought for shure I was going to get home again. But we left Sunday night + went to Staten Island VIA train +Ferry. Then we got on our transport the S.S. Marine Devil. There we had 2 weeks of rest. I didn't get as sick as I did in the East River. We came over in a pretty big convoy with plenty of D.E.s (Destroyer Escort boats) around. We landed 2 weeks later at La Havre after one night in Weymouth England. At La Havre we seen our first wrecked city. Well after a day we got off the Ship + go to the train + get in these 40 or 80 boxcars. (I thought I would freeze). Well we ride for 2 days + nights + told we are going right in combat as replacements to clean up in Southern Germany. But somebody must have changed there mind so we get off at MunchenGladback+ lay around there a week+ all at once there are a whole bunch of trucks to pick us up + take us to our outfit. So we all pile on bag and baggage + go to Lindel + join the 106th Division which is assigned to the 15th Army. I am attached to the 106th Division but unassigned (there insignia is round with a red ring then a white ring + a blue back ground with a lions head).

(So at Lindel we take showers in a big coal mine) In a couple of Days we go to Riech, Germany + spend the night + now we are in a little town named Whitcraft.

Now I am guarding German P.W. (Prisoners of War) we got

about 40,000 here. Once in a while they try to escape but somebody is generally around to pop them off. I think we will stay here as the Army of Occupation.

I am situated in the Rhine Valley

I will write more later but I need some writing papers if you can get any and how about a package of eats

I will try to write to Gram Glover + Macomber if I have time.

Write soon + don't worry everything is fine. I got here at the right time.

Give my regards to everybody.

The Hitler-led German government was formally abolished through the signing of the 1945 Berlin Declaration (later ratified at the Potsdam conference), where the four Allied powers divided Germany into four occupation zones for administrative purposes.

The Army of the Occupation was the term used to refer to the United States military organizations responsible for government authority in one of the four designated territories of the former German Reich.

One of the controversial moments of the plan occurred when the USSR complained that the US Army, during the final weeks of the war, had pushed as much as two hundred miles east beyond their zone's boundaries. The United States agreed in July 1945 to withdraw and move within the boundaries as agreed by the Allied powers.

May 23. Germany

Received your first letter today dated May 7. I shure was glad to get it. You said you didn't get any mail yet but it's coming because I wrote every 2 or 3 days

> *Just heard censorship has been lifted*
>
> *I'm guarding German P.W. (Prisoners of War) at Whitcraft it is near Munchen Gladback (Monchengladboch)*
>
> *It is between Dusseldorf, Aachen +Cologne. Everything is ruined. Aachen is a pretty large city + there is only a couple of Smoke stacks standing*
>
> *Will write more later.*

By the end of the war, the original purpose of censorship—to eliminate potentially important military information accidentally sent through the mail—was no longer necessary. The military realized that after May 1945, most of the censors were reading private letters that were completely unrelated to military activities. A censor reported a humorous example of such a letter when a solder wrote to his girlfriend back home that he was very angry with his wife for dating another man. As a result, it was decided that there was little value in continuing to censor soldiers' letters home.

The envelope for the May 23 letter contained a second letter.

Dear Mr. and Mrs. Glover

Well I suppose you are wondering who is writing you this letter well I'll try and explain in as few words as possible. Well me and your son Bob are very good pals and we are in the same room we sleep together so he told me so much about you it would really be a pleasure meeting you and your family. Mrs. Glover when we boys start talking about our girlfriends back home we always ask Bob about his and he say his mother is his best girl so you see Mrs. Glover if your Bob's best girl you really must be swell. I hope you don't mind me writing you. You see we have nothing to do at the present time and I have Bob's permission

Well Mrs. Glover you see me and bob went through basic training together. I was planning to come over when we went on fourlough but I had lost his address. So I'll sign off for now with my best regards to the family especially the two little ones.

Just another soldier

Will

PS Please try to write

Bob's many letters from home impressed his friends. Europe was a long way from home and a lonely place for many, so letter writing was one of the few ways soldiers could stay in touch with civilians, or "normal people." Bob gave his buddies permission to write to his family and encouraged them to do so, knowing that it would provide his mother with a new source of entertainment. Whilden "Will" wrote again a few months later.

The Battle of Aachen occurred several months earlier, in October 1944. In September, initial fighting had caused Aachen's city commander to surrender the city to the advancing Americans. However, the German SS discovered his letter of surrender as the civilians evacuated the city. Upon discovery of the impending surrender, Hitler ordered the immediate arrest of the city commander and sent Gerhard Wilck's 246th Volksgrenadier Division to resist the Allied incursion.

The American commanders decided to surround the city and use the 1st and 30th Infantry Divisions to capture Aachen. Aerial and artillery bombardment failed to inflict major damage on German defenses, and the division's strike against the German defenses in the north got bogged down. The First Army suffered 5,000 casualties in Aachen, and the Germans suffered an estimated 5,000 casualties and another 5,600 soldiers taken prisoner. As Bob passed through the city, he was able to observe firsthand the devastating results of the bombing.

Germany Friday, May 25, 1945

Dear Butch + Janet,

Well butch I have (n't) written to you in a long time. I've had plenty of time but just never got around to it. I am in the best of health + hope this letter finds you under the same circumstances. I'll bet you + Janet will be a young man + lady when I get home. You had better write me + tell me how you are making out in school.

Well I'll sign off but don't forget to write.

May 25

Dear Doll,

Well, Well Well. I bet scared and I mean Scared you. Don't be frightened though its only your brother writing a V-mail form.

Wait till I get home this time all shaped up. I am shure of the E.T.O. Ribbon (European Theater of Operations)

With one battle star for being here on V. E. Day and no telling how many gold bar on my sleeve.

I'll bet you + Carl had a big time on that glorious day.

Note the Hdq. in return address it means Headquarters Company. You can just imagine what kind of a good outfit this is with me in Headquarters. No kidding this is a darn good outfit. I like to write the word Headquarters because it takes up so much room. (!)

love

Bob

The Bronze Star medal was awarded to members of the 106th ID. The Bronze Star is the fourth-highest individual military award and is given for acts of heroism, merit, or service in a combat zone. During the war, Bob was proud of his award, but humble, claiming he didn't deserve it and that he had arrived in Europe after the "real fighting" was over.

After his return to civilian life, he never spoke about it.

May 25 Friday Germany.

. . . Everything is O.K., only thing happened is I had some bad luck yesterday + broke my watch strap + catch on my bracelet.

We are taking it easy most of the time over here.

I am now in a room with a fellow who used to work in the Washington Navy Yard . . .

By the start of WWII, the Washington Navy Yard, located in Washington, DC was the largest naval ordnance plant in the world. At its peak, the Yard consisted of 188 buildings on 126 acres and employed nearly 25,000 people. It was designated a National Historic Landmark in 1976.

May 25 Friday Germany.

. . . We got 2 free bottles of Coca Cola yesterday. It tasted darn good.

They have a movies here + a show about every night. When we aren't doing any –thing we go . . . last night we saw Laura+ the other night we seen Now Tomorrow . . . both were pretty good.

We get our laundry done for 2 ½ marks . . . is $.25. They also have some German beer which is 3 glasses for one mark the only trouble is the beer isn't any good . . . I will try to write Charlie a letter now

---

May 27, Germany

Dear Dad,

Well I hope you are feeling fine +not working to hard.

Me + another boy have gotten together + become pretty good pals. He used to be an electrician in the Norfolk Navy Yard.

Last night being Saturday he + I started for the Donut Dugout about 10 miles away in another town it was about 7 o'clock when we started. So we got a ride about halfway in a truck + before we knew it it was 9 o'clock + the place closed at 9 so we started back + couldn't get a ride for nothing. It finally got dark + cloudy+ when we come to a village we could feel about 20 guns in our back. I wouldn't have minded getting shot at but we were mad because we didn't get the donuts.

We read about the Franklin coming in.

Hope everybody is O.K.

Love,

Bob

In 1945, for safety and security reasons, General Eisenhower ordered the confiscation of all privately owned firearms in the American-occupied zones in Germany. German citizens were required to hand in all shotguns and rifles. The US soldiers were amazed when they discovered that the vast number of German citizens owned firearms. The Soviets were considered much more aggressive than Eisenhower in their control of non-military weapons; they simply shot any civilian found with even a single cartridge.

Bob's reference to the USS *Franklin* came as a result of the recent news coverage of the damage the ship had suffered in the Pacific. The USS *Franklin*, one of twenty-four aircraft carriers built for the US Navy during World War II, was named for

Benjamin Franklin and saw significant action in the Pacific, earning four battle stars.

In March 1945 the *Franklin* suffered heavy damage from a Japanese air attack, losing over eight hundred members of its crew. (Movie footage of the actual attack can be seen in the Gary Cooper movie *Task Force*). Following the attack, the ship returned to the Brooklyn Navy Yard on 28th April 1945 via the Panama Canal for much needed repairs. She was decommissioned in 1947 and sold for scrap in 1966.

Roy was continuing to work in the Brooklyn Navy Yard. Years later, Bob learned that his father had gotten into some trouble shortly before the war's end, partially because he was fiercely proud of his son and partially because he was proud of the US Army's efforts in Europe. During the war, the Yard employed thousands of workers from many backgrounds and nationalities. During breaks, the work crews discussed a variety of subjects, including sports, politics, and of course, the war. One hot day in 1945, several workers brought up the subject of the Selective Service draft process and contrasted it to voluntary enlistment. At that time, it was under debate whether men should enlist, as the war was winding down and recruitment efforts had slowed. Roy mentioned that his son, Bob, had enlisted in late 1944. A few workers teased Roy, pointing out that many sons of celebrities were known not to have qualified for battle status like Bob had. What began as friendly teasing evolved into a debate about the wisdom—or lack thereof—of the men who would volunteer at this point in the war. Roy felt that several of the workers had crossed the line with their comments. One man kept goading Roy, saying, "What the heck would your son do a fool thing like that for? Didn't he know what he was getting into?" That was the last straw; the usually gregarious Roy was now livid, and he aimed his rivet gun at the man's head, as if intending to plant a rivet in his coworker's skull. Of course, a fight ensued, but was quickly broken up by others among them.

The passage of time has made it difficult to determine who was and who was not arrested, but it's likely that the subject of enlistment wasn't brought up again at work in Roy's presence.

May 30, Germany

Dear Mom

Today I received a letter from you + Butch.

Glad to hear that you are getting mail about the Army of Occupation. I don't believe I will get in it. Hope you had a happy birthday.

I would like to know what hospital Sylvester is in maybe I'll get a chance to see him.

You say don't get friendly with any of these people. Well if we do it costs us $65 for fraternizing.

I didn't get any package yet +I don't know if I ever will if we keep moving around.

Keep those letters coming.

The US military commanders had proactively enacted a fraternization ban in 1944, well before V-E Day. The ban was partially driven by the need to demonstrate publicly that the US military was taking a tough stance toward all Germans. The ban prohibited US military personnel from taking part in any activities that involved German civilians.

American soldiers, away from home for long periods of time, were tempted to communicate with German civilians—particularly German women. If caught, a soldier might face up to six months in confinement and a loss of up to two-thirds of one's pay.

Over time, it became difficult for the Army to enforce the ban; soldiers objected to the ban, particularly when it came to children, who the soldiers could more easily bond and communicate with, but the Army held firm. When soldiers complained that it was difficult for them to distinguish between Germans, French, or Poles, military commanders experimented with methods of easily identifying different nationalities. One experiment required for civilians to wear colored armbands and buttons, but this quickly proved to be a foolish endeavor, and also a curiously familiar one.

General Eisenhower realized the challenge of continued enforcement of the ban, and on July 15th, he revised the order to allow soldiers to mingle with civilians.

JUNE 1945—COBLENZ, ONE YEAR AFTER D-DAY

June 5 Germany

Turned in $100 for a money order when I get the money order I will send it.

Rumors are flying thick + fast about coming home. They range from tomorrow till July 15th so there must be something in it, as for myself I would just as leave stay here a year or two+ come home because if we come home now we will get about 30 days + then go to the C. B. I.

Training still goes on . . .

The name of that city we are near is Coblenz.

I think about home a lot. There is a 6 hr. difference so we have done a half day's work (+ I mean work climbing over the mountains) before you get up. It don't get dark around here till 10 (11?) P.M. is light at about 4.

Well that's enough bolongie for today. See you soon.

Despite the fact that the war in Europe was formally ended, the US military still needed personnel for the Army of the Occupation, and for conflicts in other parts of the world—such as Japan and the China-Burma-India conflict. Soldiers who did not have enough points to qualify for return to the United States were considered to fill these roles.

China Burma India Theater (CBI, later referred to as IBT, or India-Burma Theater) was the name used by the US Army for its forces operating in conjunction with the British and Chinese Allied air and land forces in China, Burma, and India during World War II.

June 6 Germany

Well one year ago was D day so we get a half a day of training off but have a night problem tonight.

It shure is getting hot over here

Rumors are flying fast as ever about coming home

. . . I think air mail goes as fast as V mail if not faster.

In case you don't know it this 106 Div. was wiped out in the Belgium break though + it still isn't straightened out

. . . Tell Dad that the fellow he met at the bus station is still with me only in K Co. of the same Reg.

Before you get this letter I will have been away 2 months. Dad said I'd see some of the world well tell him I've seen enough.

I remember a year ago today I was making gas tanks in the Navy Yard.

I hope it don't take to long to whip Japan because I am getting more discusted with this army every day.

They are letting most of the German P.W go home.

Every time I write a letter I get hungry, boy I could go for one of your lamb /ham (?) sandwiches with a quart of cold milk.

That bag you + Dolly bought me shure did come in handy. I've carried my toilet articles in it ever since+ I wouldn't have anything else to put them in.

These Germans are ready to fight again only this time us and them against Russia. Every one of them are afraid of the Russians.

They have hooked up a radio to a loud speaker in the woods here + we get the states once in a while.

I often wonder how . . . (you are all) doing . . . how is that old

> *man Conn making out?*
>
> *We just had supper had Lamb Stew, Beets, Dehardrated Carrot, Choclate pudding, 4 small hard candies, bread + coffee*
>
> *I read in the stars +Stripes where they are short of meat home don't let that worry you because for breakfast I had a tablespoon of dehydrated eggs and 4 raisins.*
>
> *Do you hear any news from Cutchogue? . . . Dont worry about nothing everything is all set*

Now that the fighting was ended in Europe, Army mess halls were able to set up field facilities and could prepare higher quality meals. These were considered by the soldiers to be much better than the rations provided during the war. Bob's supper would have been considered a feast by the Glover family at home. He was wise to preface the passage by reassuring his mother that her sandwiches were foremost on his mind.

> *June 8th Germany.*
>
> *Yesterday Got 14 letters from you . . . 1 ½ to 2 months old.*
>
> *Didn't write yesterday because we had a 24 hr. problem. I guess I will get mail from you regular now.*
>
> *Well I just got 5 more points to make a total of 11, two May 12 for these, 5 for a bronze star which all of us in the company got for fighting at Lortienz France. Don't be mistaken I wasn't there but I get a bronze star anyhow because this company gets one.*
>
> *Tell Carl + Dolly that here is a word we use over here for plenty . . . it is (Boo-Coo).*
>
> *It seems funny to me I live in the woods out in the rain + everything else+ I don't get sick. (Please explain)*
>
> *Don't forget to let me know about the money order + Bonds*

+Don't forget to pay the insurance. I'm glad now that we kept the insurance.

Oh yes I am the ammo. Bearer for the B.A. R. in our squad.

We only are supposed to have 4 more weeks of training + then we go to the C.B. I. directed or by way of U.S. let's hope I come home again. We aren't in a hurry to do either.

I hope I get your package tonight.

June 10 Sunday Germany

. . . just got back from taking a shower they took us in trucks about 15 miles.

I hope Butch gets over his whooping cough soon . . . tonight I got motor pool guard so I'll have a half a day off tomorrow

When we go through a town + I see there Germans home + eating homemade bread I feel envious.

We had chicken for dinner.

Last night we had some champaing + conyack, you know the stuff you drink. The champaing is good but the other stuff isn't much good.

June 10 Monday Germany

. . . I got off till 10 o'clock because I had guard last night.

Got our P.X. rations the other day we got 6 packs cigarettes 5 candy bars + 1 bar of soap for a week.

We had 3 pancakes for breakfast.

Ask Charley how long he thinks the war with Japan will last.

I read in the Stars + Stripes where they are going to occupy Germany for 20 yrs. So I wouldn't want to get in that because it would probably be 5 yrs. for me . . .

June 8 Germany

To Mr. R. P. Glover

Dear Butch.

I just got a letter from Mom saying that you were sick well you had better get well quick because I've got a possible chance of coming home soon.

Tell Mom she wonders how I like it over here. Well there isn't nothing this the U. S.

Hurry up + get well + when I come home we'll just eat cherry pie, milk,+ candy.

June 16th (labeled Saturday) Germany

Well you'll have to excuse me for not writing for a few days but I've been so discusted with the mail situation. Haven't got any in a week now + I know it has had time to catch up to me.

I hope Butch is O.K. now ...

We had a parade this afternoon makes you feel good to parade in front of these Germans.

Enclosed is our shoulder patch it is the 106th Div.

You can send a package ... still didn't get any yet ...

Demobilization of the US military in Europe following WWII became a difficult balancing act for the War Department. It asked the question of how many troops should be sent home and when. Troops were still needed to perform the administrative and police duties required to manage the civilian population.

It was an enormous task to plan for and manage the processing of three million US soldiers in Europe. The military commanders decided to send one million men from Europe to the

Pacific to fight in Asia; they would send the remaining two million men to the United States over a period of time. This required a colossal amount of planning and eventually resulted in confusion for everyone.

On January 4, 1946, the War Department realized that more soldiers were needed to perform postwar activities in Europe than originally planned, resulting in the delayed return for thousands of soldiers, sparking confusion and protests among the enlisted men.

Eventually, the military planners got it right. The total number of US military enlisted personnel dropped from 12 million to 1.5 million between mid-1945 and mid-1947.

June 16th Sunday Germany

Dear Butch + Janet,

Glad to get your letters + hope you both are fine.

I am enclosing you + Janet some invasion money worth 10 cents a peace some French + German money

Maybe I'll be home pretty soon you cant tell what they are going to have us do it says in the paper it is a secret assignment.

Well you two take care of yourself_ eat some candy + Ice Cream for me

---

Bob had mailed home what was commonly known as "invasion money."

During the preparation for the D-Day invasion of German-occupied France, the Allies planned to print and issue special currency, named "French" currency. The goal was to support devalued French banknotes and to act as payment for Allied troops and citizens stationed in France. American servicemen, stationed in England prior to D-Day, were paid in British pounds; they surely would have preferred French currency when they landed in

France. Nineteen trucks were required to deliver three billion French francs—the estimated amount necessary to change out the British money held by American servicemen into French Military Currency.

June 17 Sunday

Got Bookoo mail today 20 letters but still no package. They have been bringing me some Glovers package from Oregon, so maybe he is getting mine.

I feel a lot better that I got mail again.

Still is pretty cold here in the morning.

Yesterday we had a Regimental parade it makes you feel pretty good to march around in front of these God Damn Germans.

They have put up a great big flag pole with the American Flag on it + it makes you feel pretty good to see it.

You would be surprised of how many friends you can make in 2 weeks all the guys in the Company are just like brothers . . . treat you swell.

Got letters from carl + every body Jean, Gram, Butch, Janet, Doll, you + Mrs. Newsom

Don't forget to let me know about the money order + the bonds + Don't forget to pay the insurance.

What happened to the pictures I had taken . . . I get a letter from Clair I look like a movie actor.

How about sending some pictures of you people to me I still got the other ones but I could use some more

I don't remember if I asked you for a watch strap or not but if I didn't . . . send one because I got my watch tied to my pants with a piece of string.

Tell Butch to tell Dad I am in the 106th Div.

It said in the Stars + Stripes that the 15th Army has a Secret assignment —that's us. Hope it has something to do with the states.

You don't appreciate the states till you are away from them

We are now getting 10% more food they get us champaign + cognac + beer . . . living in the woods you appreciate little things like that even if the beer + cognac isn't any good.

Did I ever tell you about going to Camp Shanks + staying 23 hrs. I was so close home + yet so far away. We left from Staten Island.

When I get home again you are going to have to learn me to sew.

I bet you will be having leg of lamb today I could go for some lamb with mashed potatoes and peas.

PS: Air Mail is better . . . don't say I didn't request anything. I have requested pictures + a watch strap

June 19 Tuesday Germany

Received a letter from Janet and Jean yesterday it took them only 10 days to get there by airmail

Today they started to talk about August so there is no telling how long we might be here. The 1st of August they are going to start us on that athletic+ Education coarce. that will be a heck of a lot better than what we are doing now.

. . . I pretty near forgot my pass come through it is either thursday or Saturday for 3 days but it will take 8 or 9 days after traveling time is included

We are going to the Reveria, Brussels, Paris or Namur Belgium most likely the latter.

I only had $11 so I borrowed $20 so I won't be able to send any

> *home next month . . .*
>
> *What gives with the Whooping cough?*
>
> *Tell Daddy to take all the days he can get off + Don't sleep in to obvious places on the boats.*
>
> *What's the matter Carl gone crazy again sailing to Greenport.*
>
> *We are getting better eats now with the 10% increase.*
>
> *I laugh at these guys about 30 years old who get together + worry about there lives after the war.*
>
> *P.S. Hope you can read it*

Bob's remark about Carl is another example of Bob's dislike. Carl enjoyed sailing and occasionally convinced Bob's sister Dolly to sail off on impromptu trips in the Peconic Bay. This was worrisome to Louise and Roy; Bob knew that and was gently reminding them of Carl's behavior.

> *June 20 Germany*
>
> *Well I leave Friday night for my pass + wont get back till next Wednesday. I am going to Namur Belgium.*
>
> *That's good news but I also have some bad rumors that all fellows with under twenty five points will go direct to the Pacific but its only another rumor. At times you shure do get discussed but so of the fellows who have been in for four years are the ones who should be.*
>
> *Maybe someday I'll get my package.*
>
> *Nothing new except a lot of rumors.*
>
> *Lots of Love*

June 21 Germany

Well today was the longest day of the year + I am still sweating out the packages.

Did pretty good on mail though received 3 letters from You, Doll + Carl. Your's + Carl's were old but Dolly's was June 4th.

Dolly asked about the German soldiers. Well they run from 11 to 60. They are Civilians Russian, French, Polish + every other kind of nationality that they made fight.

The Prison Camp that I was at was about 1 mile by 1 mile with triple barbed wire fence all around.+ on the inside of the tripple fence they had them in separate pens but they still got out.

We used to have a great time when they would bring them in on box cars + then 4 of us would take from 400 to 600 of them + march them 2 miles to the camp. They would try to lag behind so they could get a chance to make a break but we would persuade them to go on either by your foot or the butt of your gun + the streets used to be lined with civilians trying to give them something to eat.

We had a couple of cases where the civilians met some relative in the parade.

After we got them by the camp we would have to search every one of them + put them in. About one out of every ten can speak good English + every once in a while you would meet a guy who had been to the United States. Some of the boys got addresses that the Germans gave them in the States.

Dolly said Carl's Uncle was in well maybe I butted him along +tell her I cant trust the Females because I cant even talk to them without it costing me $125 + 3 months of hard labor.

Will + I got separated he is in another Regiment now but his last name is Guadanago. He lives on the other side of the G. W.

Bridge.

Don't forget to send the pictures

Hope you all get well because you cant tell what might happen, even though that rumor about going straight to the Pacific is strong, I might get home.

Keep your eyes open in the paper about the 15th Army + the 106 Div. It is generally in the states papers before we know it.

Don't worry about nothing. If they do start us on our way to the Pacific it will take 3 or 4 months.

Tomorrow night I start my pass at 2 o'clock some of the boys who (went) there for 3 days spent from 84 to 300 dollars because everything is so high, so you can imagine what a time I am going to have with $30.

Let me know how my affairs (circled in dots) are. Did you get the money order? Did you pay the insurance?

If we are here August 1st we start this HE coarce it is like going to school. Information+ Education. That will be a heck of a lot better than running over these mountains . . . it is cold at night + hot in the day time . . . Don't forget to send the pictures

Every time I see a little German I tell him if he starts anything I will get my kid brother to take care of him. Tell that to Butch it will make him feel good

See that I write to much when I get plenty of mail.

Will write more tomorrow before I leave if I have time

Lots of Love

PS: Request. Send something to eat.

Note. Me + Dad hit our Vacation together only 4000 miles apart.

When POWs were processed in the camps, they were required to provide their names and home addresses. Bob was surprised that some of the German POWs were so familiar with the United States that instead of a providing a German address, they actually gave an American one! It is likely that the POWs were trying to establish a common ground between them and the American soldiers in the hope of getting special treatment.

Guadango was one of Bob's Army buddies who lived in New Jersey. Following the war, the two spoke over the phone on rare occasions, but never met up.

June 22 Germany

Well tonight at 2 I am leaving on my pass to Belgium where I am going is only 40 miles from Brussels so I guess I can make it there. Wont be back till next Wednesday so maybe I will get some rest

Some of the boys say you can get Ice Cream there+ Strawberry Shortcake only trouble is that everything is so high.

I am sending 5 francs note worth about 12 cents a franc is worth about 2 ¼ cents.

PS: . . . Don't expect no mail for a couple of Days.

June 28, Thursday Germany

It(s) raining just as hard as possible + I got a moat around my pup tent like a castle.

Got back 8 o'clock this morning from my pass had a good time. We started at 2 Sat. morning + went to Bonn, Germany by truck and after a wait we catch a broken down old train + go to Leige, Bel. + after another wait we take off for Namur. It's a pretty good size city + it is located on some river or canal. So after seeing Namur which isn't much Monday 3 of us catch a train for

---

Brussels. Now that is a nice city. Somewhat like New York + is banged up much. We stayed there until Wed. morning + went back to Namur.

I bought a handkerchief in Brussels for you which is enclosed it cost 35 Francs so you can see what inflation they have. That is about 79 or 80 cents. We had Boo Coo ice cream any way + here is something else I have to tell you + tell this to Dolly. 3 of us with our dirty clothes, collar open + hat on the backs of our heads go into one of these high class joints + we order a steak dinner + they started to cook it we get a tip that it costs over a 1000 Francs for the 3 of us so we call back the waiter + tell him Chicken Dinner so after a ½ hr. wait with all these high class Belguims looking at us + us watching what they eat the waiter comes with 2 small chickens + starts tearing then apart + we watch him giving him a little advice. He gives us each a peace +Some French Fries so I eat the fries and we can't decide how you should eat chicken so I pick up my piece with my finger + eat it + the other guys did the same. So the waiter rushes over + gives us each another piece + before he can get back to his corner he comes + gives us another piece. Well with some Strawberries with whipped cream it cost us each 320 francs anyway.

While I was there I got myself a strap for my watch + a cigarette lighter + a knife so I am satisfied.

We have started real maneuvers with airplanes dropping flour + tanks running all over. I hope this will finish our training.

Division to go home + to the pacific have been moved up till August + it said the 106th is temperorly occupying + awaiting further orders so I hope it is true. The 15th Army (that's us) is supposed to have some secret assignment. I hope it is occupying the States for about 1 yr . . . Well I guess I'll catch up on my sleep.

Bob was commenting about two important issues that would eventually affect all of Europe. He was surprised in regard to the inflated prices for the meal, and was surprised at the availability of beef and chicken in the restaurant.

At the end of WWII, most of Europe was undergoing a period of serious monetary inflation, which resulted in the precipitous rise in prices for goods and services. The rapidly increasing food prices were a clear indication of how dangerous the situation had become. In some corners of Europe, people who couldn't afford to buy food were slaughtering and eating their pets.

Hyperinflation was a significant concern. Hungary was an extreme example, suffering the highest recorded inflation ever. Between August 1945 and July 1946, the rate of inflation was estimated at 41.9 quintillion percent—an astounding number!

In Europe, it was estimated that since the beginning of the war, food production had been reduced by half. Many of the farmers who grew or produced food had been killed or crippled. To manage food inventories during the war, Hitler had begun a policy of food rationing, which limited food intake for the general population.

After the war, the Allies had little alternative but to continue to reinforce this policy of food rationing. Price controls on food, goods, and services were announced, leading to more shortages and the creation of a black market where such goods could be sold. The Germany currency, the Reichsmark, was virtually worthless, making it necessary to barter for goods and services.

Bob's waiter was likely happy to cater to the soldiers' requests for more food and was likely charging the soldiers a premium for their meal. It was also likely that the chicken was purchased on the black market. The Belgian government was proactive in their attempts to control inflation, and in 1946, the government froze wages and imposed a ten percent reduction in prices to curb inflation.

June 28 Thursday Germany

Today I got 4 letters + the Mirror . . . still feeling fine and wish all of you would get better. Had a detail today + tomorrow with guard duty tonight. These details are O.K. They at least keep you from playing Cops + Robbers.

We are fixing up a place here in a German school house (smaller than E. C. S.) for the Red Cross so they can start making us donuts+ coffee. You buy 12 coupons for 10 cents + you get a cup of coffee for 2 coupons and 1 coupon per donut. The only trouble is you can't buy but 2 donuts at a time.

. . . They are letting plenty of guys go on passes now + still fixing up everything so maybe we will stay here till Dec. I hope so.

I am bunking with a guy now who's brother was killed in Italy 1 mo before the war was over + now 2 of his 3 sisters got married so he is pretty burnt up.

I'm sorry to hear about all the ships getting damaged by . . . somebody has got to fight the Japs + the Navy is just the guys far as I'm concerned

Did you read where this Admiral says they should send the infantry in + clean them out? Well let the navy help this time.

If a fellow can live to get 85 points in the Infantry he's lucky. These guys here are pretty burnt up at this Admiral.

I cant catch no canaries here haven't even seen one

You had all better take a vacation and go to the country.

We're still on maneuvers they have a 36 hr. problem tomorrow + Sat afternoon a parade

I don't get tired of reading any of your letters

PS: Still no package

Make sure you put the right address on them.

June 29 Friday Germany

. . . I have been working up at the Red Cross.

At Late mail call yesterday o received another Mirror + a letter from You + Doll both of them had pictures in them.

Butch + Janet are getting tall. You +Doll look the same except for Doll on the Merry-go –Round + there she looks like a young kid. You look just the same as the picture I have of you which was taken in 1940.

Glad you got the money order + I hope you didn't have any trouble cashing it.

By the way where is Indian's Point?

I guess I'll sigh off + (Coo-shay) Sleep.

Bob had not seen his family in more than six months, so Butch, eight years old, and Janet, ten years old, had most likely grown. Bob certainly knew how to flatter his mother, suggesting that she looked the same as she did five years ago.

June 30 Sat. Germany

Well today I worked on the Red Cross detail again. Got our candy rations + are supposed to get paid so everything was O.K.

. . . 2 Varga girls were here today for supper + they are putting on a show at The Copa-Cabana tonight.

Got to do a lot of washing tomorrow . . . guess these letters are getting pretty dull . . . got 12 hours sleep in the rain last night . . .

"Vargas Girls" was a term used to describe the art of the Peruvian artist Joaquin Alberto Vargas y Chávez. His work was used by the Ziegfeld Follies and Hollywood studios.

In the 1940s, Vargas became famous as the creator of many iconic World War II-era pinups for *Esquire Magazine* known as "Vargas Girls." His art was adapted for use by United States airmen on World War II aircraft. Bob was referring to the models and dancers that posed for Vargas.

JULY 1945—HEIDELBERG, ETO RIBBON

July 1, 1945, Germany

Dear Mrs. Glover (mom)

I received your most welcome letter some time ago but due to circumstances I didn't have time to answer. I'm really sorry but we were pretty busy. Well mom bob and are I separated and as yet I haven't heard from him. You see I was shipped out to a different company and he stayed. Say mom I hope you don't mind me calling you mom you see when I was with Bob we always talk about you and your family and from what Bob tell me you have a great family. Well mom you sure made me feel good when you asked me to send you a request of a package but I really don't want to put you through the trouble thanks a million anyway. Say mom, you know when Bob wrote home and said to ask you youngest daughter to write to this fellow Izzy Grasso well he thought Bob meant your oldest girl. Well me and bob had a great laugh over that. Oh! Man the next time you write send me bob('s) address so I can write to him please and please forgive me for the paper but it is all I have and now I'll sign with my best regards to the family and especially you

P.S. I thank you very much for the 2 airmail stamps. I know somebody is thinking of the boys over here.

My correct address is:

> *Pvt E. A. Guadagno 42147639*
> *Can .Co 3 Inf. Regt.*
> *APO 408 c/o Postmaster*
> *NY, NY.*

Your 2nd Doughboy (I hope)

Willy

July 4 Germany

. . . I finally got the packages . . . one with socks + the other with eats. . . those socks sure come in handy. . . I received a letter from joan but none from you for 3 or 4 days. The only reason I can think of is you have gone to Cutchogue.

I hope all of you have gone to Cutchogue for a vacation.

God knows you'll get plenty of rest there.

July 7 Germany.

. . . one of the fellows just reminded me that fathers day has passed tell him I'm sorry I forgot, but I couldn't have got him anything anyhow.

Just drew numbers for passes + in 8 weeks I'll get one for Paris or England if I'm here.

Just picked up the money order for $100 which is enclosed let me know as soon as you get it.

Well that's enough for today.

Bob's experience during the Great Depression taught him how to earn, save, and invest his money wisely. Being keenly aware of the military's position forbidding the use of US dollars in Europe, and concerned about the wisdom of carrying large amounts of money with him, he decided to send his money home for safekeeping.

"Joan" is a reference to Bob's cousin, Joan Macomber.

July 9 Monday

Received a letter from you yesterday with the watch strap. Thanks a lot. I had bought one over here but it was no good.

Today they presented me with an E.T.O. ribbon.

I seen a poor kid shoot himself in the hand today with a revolver + I never heard such screaming. But it was his own fault because he was suppose to have any ammo.

I was showing the pictures round today + everybody says Daddy looks like a detective + say Butch looks like me + is quiet.

Everybody that wants doll's address I give them Janets

Just for curiosity how much money have I in the bank? If + when I get home I'm going to have a hell of a time

I am getting the bonds checked on but they say don't worry because it takes up to 6 months to get them + then you will get them all at once.

Took a shower yesterday they have a place fixed up by a stream.

I cant get to Arthur because we are on the alert for shipment + I can leave the company area but I am going to write a letter to him. I'd like to see him.

When you are around Max's the tailor see if he has heard anything about Bud or Paul + give him my regards. Tell him the Irishman + the Dutchman.

I don't believe you could ever find a better friend than Paul was even with his big ears. Maybe he is laying over here some place.

If my letters ever stop you'll know I'm moving.

These guys here kid me about Jap bait but they all feel sorry for me or something because they have been through It. They'll sit + try to explain things to you for hrs.

I run out of airmail stamps and cant get any.

PS Don't send any more packages.

The ETO Ribbon was awarded to those who served in Central Europe between March 22, 1945 and May 11, 1945.

Bob was unsure at this point about his future in the Army; he and his buddies did not know where they would be sent next: the CBI conflict, the Pacific, or home. This is the primary reason why he suggested his family refrain from sending any packages; he knew that he could be shipped out at any time and any important items addressed to him in Germany would not be forwarded to him.

July 11 Wednesday

. . . I have been sending Free mail . . . I got the watch strap

Don't send any more packages until further notice.

I have 10 minutes (to) mail this letter then mail is going to stop for a couple of weeks, that is because of our move coming up. I'll sign off now and don't worry if you don't hear from me.

July 12 Wednesday

They must have postponed our move because they tell us we can still write

I received another package yesterday . . . + 2 birthday cards.

Glad to hear you are getting the bonds, I guess that one was for May.

We had an easy day today + even saw a movies in the afternoon the name was Marriage is a Private Affair.

. . . your letters are only taking 6 days to get hear. I sure hope Carl made it to Greenport

---

July 13 Germany

We have been having it easy last couple of days. Tonight at 3 we attack another Bn. (battalion) about 20 miles from here.

Well now we hear the 28th Division is all full+ started home. I'm glad I didn't get in that because it fought to much.

The latest tip we got is the rest of the Division that goes to the States will be held in reserve there+ might not even see the Pacific.

They tell us this Hidelburg we are going near is across the river from France + that we will have some maneuvers against the 84th Div.

News about the C.B. I. sounds good over here.

They are sending about 1 fellow a week with over 85 points home from here.

I met Arthur at the Red Cross yesterday . . .

My watch is still running fine.

The 15th I will have been away from the states 3 months it seems like 3 years.

July 15 Sunday Germany

. . . they have stopped our mail till we get to our next place didn't get any for 3 days.

Everything here is the same

Three months ago today I got on the boat in Staten Island.

Me + the kid dad met from Bklyn hang around together in our time off + you can generally find us playing Ping Pong at the Red Cross eating donuts

. . . We are going to have a company picture taken after.

July 18 Germany

. . . Still expecting to get transferred any day + start home. I hope.

. . . I thought I would be home for my birthday. This will be my first birthday away from home + I hope it is the last.

July 21 Germany

Well we arrived here in Heidelberg yesterday. The whole division is located around here. On the lot we are on the whole Regiment is together. Arthur is only a couple hundred yards away.

Received 3 packages . . . 2 with plenty of candy + peanut butter + one with writing paper. Thanks a lot.

When we got here we had a company formation + the C.O. told us that we are not going to break up but stick together for some reason but some of the men will leave —Hope I am one.

At 4:30 this morning they pulled a raid on the Germans here searching all houses + persons.

They say there is still plenty of Nazi loose here.

They have relaxed the Fraternization, you can talk to the Germans in public places.

There are also plenty of misplaced persons around here. They are the people who were hitlers slaves I guess. They say every one of them has got thyphus.

I think that we are pretty near Switzerland. May I will get a pass there.

Everything is all messed up + the more they tell us the more they confuse us.

One good thing we are on level ground so I don't believe there will be to rough training.

As Bob learned in boot camp, typhus is a bacterial disease spread by lice or fleas.

According to the Dr. Rath Health Foundation, many prisoners of German concentration camps were used as human guinea pigs to test new vaccines. Several attempts were made to develop a new typhus fever drug referred to as "3582." The results of the first series of tests were far from satisfactory. Of the fifty test subjects injected, fifteen died; the typhus fever drug caused severe adverse reactions among the others. It is speculated that these subjects were left to die in quarantine.

July 21 Germany

Well we have has the whole day off so I thought I would write you another letter . . . I think if it gets any hotter today I think I will fry . . . We are now living in 6 man tents+ sleeping on cots at least you can stand up once in a while.

If I stay in this outfit until August 20 we are suppose to move + be S. G. (security guards) same thing as M. P.

The war looks good from there I hope it gets over pretty soon.

If I keep fooling around over here I doubt if I shall make it to Japan+ I think Carl will just about get through his training in time to get over here + relieve me if I occupy.

Once in a while I sit + listen to some of the rumors + you have to be careful because if you listen to long you would go crazy.

Coming down we come about 100 miles along the Rhine + it looks pretty good with mountains on each side + all along they have grapes planted on the mountain sides

If you want to you can buy a cheap pen ($1.98) + send it in a small package . . . that will be my birthday present.

July 22 Germany

. . . this morning was another scorcher . . . received 3 birthday cards. . . Gram +Jean + Butch+ Janet.

Where we are now is more level ground than we were before . . . guess we are in the Rhine Valley because you can see mountains on both sides of us a couple of miles away.

It was a nice ride down here but I am still to find one of Germanys Superhighway.

All along the road you'll find kids asking for chewing gum or chocolate or ciggrete for papa.

Then you'll find some kids throwing apples at you.

The grown up people don't ask for nothing. Some of them smile others look at you with a mean look.

The American soldiers are starting to advertize all along the road. You'll see a sign: Bill's Garage 5999 miles Houston Texas, you see different signs like that all along.

During the 1940s, pen manufacturers were constantly developing new features to compete in the crowded market. Some manufacturers claimed that their pens could write under water, some claimed the pens could write upside down, and others even advertised the ability to write through ten carbon copies. The more the manufacturers advertised, the more pens they sold and prices dropped. Still, the pens were far from perfect; most used ink that faded and required a long time to dry. The biggest problem was that for the most part, all pens still leaked.

Bob's reference to a "cheap pen" for $1.98 refers to the special advertising promotion by the Parker Pen Company. During WWII, Parker Pen and other manufacturers offered pens priced affordably at $1.98 and competed aggressively for market share. In a few short years, the BIC pen from France would successfully take large pieces of the low-priced pen market from US manufacturers when they introduced their very inexpensive and innovative ball-point pen.

July 22 Germany

Dear Butch +Janet

I received your birthday card. It was very nice.

Hope both of you + Dolly are over the whooping cough . . . I am now near Heidelberg in Germany . . . Arthur Sarno lives in a tent only about 100 yds away . . . I thought they would send me home by now . . . It only takes from 10-12 days for your letters to get here.

Write soon.

Arthur Sarno was a friend of the Glover family. His family lived in the Cutchogue area.

July 24 Germany

. . . the only trouble here is it is up to about 104 degrees you just sit and sweat + inside the tents it seems twice as hot.

I guess Daddy remembers that guy he met when I was going to Ft. Meade. Well he is leaving tomorrow for someplace . . . You can start addressing your letters different now because I have finally made Private First Class. That is about $4.60 more a month.

Tonight the restriction is lifted so I guess I will go take a look at the town.

Bob's promotion to Private First Class was a welcome event in his military career. It was the second step up the army ladder in terms of rank and it came with a slight wage increase. In the Army, "enlisted" is a term used for soldiers at the lower end of the ranking system; officers have the senior positions. Ranks for enlisted men ranged from Private to Master Sergeant. Private First Class (PFC) was higher than Private, but under the rank of Sergeant.

In WWII, the majority of soldiers had Private or PFC rankings; contrary to popular belief, a promotion was not an automatic event. A promotion to PFC was decided upon by one's supervisors, referred to as noncommissioned officers (NCOs).

Bob was suggesting in a tongue-in-cheek fashion that his family should revise his title and rank on their letters addressed to him.

July 25 Germany

Well here I am trying to write another letter.

The fellow who was here with me from Bkl'yn that Daddy met has left + if he gets home he is suppose to come see you.

Just as hot as ever today you just sit in the shade + sweat to death.

We haven't done any hard training since we got here because of the heat we are suppose to go out tomorrow + come back Saturday. I hope they call it off.

Went into this town (Langbrucken) last night + the Army has taken over 4 Beer Halls, a movies + just about everything else it is a fair size town about the size of Greenport.

For 1 mark (10 cents) you can get all the beer you can drink but it taste like hard water.

The people pretty near had a riot trying to get ration tickets from the burgermaster.

The Army is worried about this typhus one of the fellows in the

---

Bn. has got it all ready so today the general was inspecting the mess kit water + we got some kind of Powder to put on out clothes + sleeping bag.

The boys are shipping out every day, if I ever do go I am not going to tell you so I will surprise you when I get home.

The mosquitos are big as airplanes here + bite like a 30 Caliber shell.

Well I shure hope everybody is O.K. home + will stay O.K. + if I come home that I am not sick again.

I certainly hope they hurry up and invade Japan.

I figure it is time to get out of the E.T.O. because if the war is over + I get caught I will be the kind of guy they will be looking for, for about 5 years of occupation

+ another thing I hope that carl don't get in the Infantry + that he gets a break but he looks more like 5 yr. bait.

How about trying to enclose a lead pencil in a letter I have nothing to write with

Always loving all of You.

July 28

Well today is my birthday+ I guess this is the first one away from home. I started it off at 12 mid attacking some woods.

We went out Thurs. noon + got back today at noon. This was a regimental combat team but all we did was walk for about 25 miles . . . another fellow is shipping out of here who was inducted with me + is suppose to come see you if he gets home.

Don't forget to send me something to eat + to write with

. . . I hope I get out of the E. T. O. pretty soon.

Loads of Love

July 28 Eve Germany

Dear Butch + Janet,

. . . received 3 letters . . . mom, you two . . . and Uncle Emil

The package that I got is very good it has candy in it. Hugs + kisses + that other stuff.

Hope you two are getting along O.K. in school.

Tell mom I cant use American money over here. The only way I can sell it so I am returning it+ you two can buy + send me some

Vaseline Hair Tonic

2 wash cloths

If you please candy + Don't forget to send me something to write with.

Lots of love from your Brother.

During the war, Vaseline ran a successful marketing campaign that targeted US soldiers. Their ads featured clean-cut men and promised that the soldiers could look more handsome if they, too, used Vaseline Hair Tonic. It didn't hurt that Cary Grant, one of the most famous actors of the day, had the same "slick" Vaseline look.

July 30

. . . yesterday was on garbage detail

You don't know one day from the next what you are doing here.

Arthur is back from his pass . . . Tell me about the Empire State bldg.

Post Scrip. Give Butch or janet this coin. + send something to eat.

The Empire State Building, in midtown Manhattan, was only a few miles south of Bob's family apartment. Completed in 1931, the 103-story building had become an icon, representing the growth and glamour of New York. On July 28, 1945, in a dense fog, a US Army bomber plane was flying over Manhattan on its way to Newark Airport. However, the weather was so poor and visibility so low, that the pilot discovered he was actually several miles away from Newark and was instead approaching La Guardia Airport. He communicated to the flight control tower by radio that he was dropping to a lower altitude to regain visibility, but as he did, he found that the plane was headed directly toward a Manhattan skyscraper. He banked the plane to avoid hitting the skyscraper, only to crash into another: the Empire State Building. The plane hit the seventy-ninth floor, killing fourteen people and injuring many more.

It must have been frightening for Bob, sitting so many miles away, to think of his family so close to danger.

July 30
This is the second letter this afternoon we had athletecs so I played Volley ball.
. . . tonight I am going to take some laundry to Langenbuicken (Langenbach) + see if some German will do it.
If you give them a bar of soap they will do it or for some candy but you still have to furnish the soap.
I'm going to put in an application for radio school it's on your own time but there isn't nothing else to do so I might as well try to get to go.
They are going to take 3 farm boys out of the Regiment to England to see how they farm

July 31

Well today is payday + there is a lot of excitement about fellows shipping every day they are shipping a bunch some place.

Maybe I'll get called one of these days. I'll get my orders + it's a fifty-fifty chance to go home or to the C. B. I. I hope I hit the right order but there is no use worrying about it.

Arthur + I went to the show last night but the mosquitos eat you up.

I ate 2 boxes of Hydrox English Style cookies last night when I come back+ I thought of all the milk I could have drunk with them.

Haven't had but dehydrated milk since I left the States.

. . . We got up at 4:00 AM this morning + went on a 10 mile hike + I fell just as good as ever.

Don't build your hopes up about me coming home because you can't tell what they might do. When I ship out the letters will stop no matter where I go so you + I will both have to wait + see. I would be willing to go direct if I could get in a service remit but if I stay in the Infantry I want to come home.

Loads of love

AUGUST 1945—ATOMIC BOMB, V-J DAY

August 1st Germany

. . . the A.P.O. moved down here with us + they stopped the mail for security.

Your mail has been getting here in 5 to 10 days I think is pretty good . . .

Jack Benny Ingrim Bergman + some other I never heard of it was pretty good

Half of the company has left + I am still left but expect to get alerted any day.

We are taking it easy now in the mornings we have a couple hours of oreantation (lectures) + in the afternoon we play ball.

Arthur is still around . . .

Probably see you soon

August 2 Germany

Still laying around having a few lectures now + then + playing ball.

Saturday we have a Divisional Parade to accept the battle colors for all these guys who got wiped out in the Bulge

About only half of this company is left + in the next couple of orders are going to Regiments that will go direct to the Pacific but will be cadre in a replacement Depot so if I get on that it wont be to bad.

Hope you are getting mail by now.

Bob's letter suggests that the US armed forces, suffering the loss of seventy-five thousand casualties during the Battle of the Bulge, continued to honor the fallen, in this situation, with a parade. History shows that the battle was also devastating for the Germans, who lost eighty thousand to one hundred thousand soldiers. It was a critical battle for the Germans, they eventually lost control of the Ardennes area.

August 5

Cant figure why you aren't getting mail . . . suppose to move in houses tomorrow

The way they are shipping out, they are going near Le Havre so maybe I'll get home next week or next year, you cant figure it out.

August 7

It looks like this occupation is a good deal. Just a couple of fellows on guard+ a few other details. This morning nobody done anything + they took the company swimming this afternoon there is a nice swimming pool near here + also a lake. If I stay here long enough maybe I'll learn to swim.

Now that we have a lot of high point men I don't think we'll get much training.

You had better send me some cigarettes because they have cut our rations down to 5 packs a week and I would like a package.

When I get home nobody had better tell me everything is going overseas because it will be tough going for them.

August 8

What do you think I made General, I am only a P.F.C. + it took an Act of Congress to do that.

> *We are living like Kings now clothes pressed + cleaned, shoes shined + everything clean the only thing that bothers me is the inspections*
>
> *. . . I am bumming around with a fellow named Aundray who has 85 points + come in this outfit from the 119 Inf. So he can go home in Nov.*
>
> *He + I were talking to a couple of German girls last night + they call themselves Hitler maidens + they claim Old Hitler isn't dead yet.*
>
> *I get a kick out of these germans who use 1 cow to pull a 2 horse wagon. Very seldom you'll see a wagon with 2 animals pulling it.*
>
> *Carl was always after me to get in the Navy we(ll) you can tell him he had better contribute himself before he gets drafted*
>
> *Heard rumors Japan was invaded.*

Members of the League of German Girls (Bund Deutscher Mädel, or BDM) continued their efforts weeks after the end of the war. It was surprising to Bob that these women would openly state that "Old Hitler isn't dead yet." He wasn't sure if they were attempting to engage him in conversation, or if they were serious.

The BDM was an organization formed by the Nazi Party for girls aged fourteen to eighteen. Another group was established for younger girls aged ten to fourteen, called the Young Girls League. Both organizations were the result of Adolf Hitler's philosophies regarding women and their impact on the long-term future of Germany. He believed that German girls needed to be trained to be healthy and strong and to become the best mothers possible. Initially, membership was voluntary, but then in the early 1930s German law banned all other youth organizations. By 1936, the BDM had become compulsory.

Much of the education and training the BDM provided focused on the skills women needed to be good wives and mothers. Camps were organized for weekends and summers, political issues like National Socialism were taught, and physical activities like long distance marches, swimming, and running were encouraged.

Once a girl completed her time in the BDM, she qualified to go to university or to get a job. But before any of these activities could take place, a girl had to provide a year of service for her country called "Landfrauenjahr"—typically a year of working on farms.

During the war, the girls performed many tasks such as: collecting old clothing, gathering paper for fuel, entertaining the troops, and helping German citizens following the Allied bombing raids.

A few months after WWII ended, the BDM was formally disbanded on October 10th 1945.

August 9 Germany Envelope Addressed to: To Miss Janet Glover

Dear Butch + Janet,

I haven't received a letter from either of you for a long time . . . I guess you are pretty busy in school.

Our company is now occupying a town larger than Greenport. We are living in the best houses + are just sitting around getting fat. If the Army was always like this it would be alright.

The name of the town is Weither all the people are farmers + all hate the Russians. We heard that the Russian declared War on Japan but we hear so many rumors you don't know what is true until a couple of days later when we get the stars + stripes

There are also a few oil wells around here that we are guarding . . . hope both of you Pass in school

Love
Bob

August 9 Germany

Dear Dad,

Well its raining + blowing out + its 2 o'clock in the afternoon + I don't go on guard till 6 so I thought I would drop you a line.

Mom told me you got on the day shift + I hope that you like it

I have been trying to get in this I+E. studies but they don't seem to want to fool around with low point men. I have put in applications for Radio School + Auto Mechanic but they seem to be picking the high point men. But when they have to get another quota I will apply again. I wish they would ask for men to go to sheet metal school then I could really write them a story.

When you put in an application you have to tell what you have done + how this training will help you. I could write a couple of pages on that + maybe they would take me.

The news sounds good over hear + maybe the war will be over one of these days.

I guess I will sign off + catch a little extra sleep +write when you have time

Love Bob

August 9 Germany

Well as you can see I received the pen + it writes good I hope you didn't pay to much for it.

It is raining and blowing just about as hard as it can I wouldn't mind that so much but I have guard tonight.

I seen in the Stars + Stripes last night where Russia has declared war on Japan. Well I guess that is going to help me out a lot . . . about this C.B.I. deal every day a couple of fellows leave for *someplace.*

All they do is come around + say you are leaving in a half hr. be ready to go so you don't know when you are going. I'm still expecting to go any day because this life is to easy to last for me.

This Atomic bomb they are using must be a great thing. But I hope they know what they are fooling with.

We had a class on these new 57mm + 75 mm guns which they have invented that don't kick for the infantry + that would help you out a hell of a lot in combat.

This company expects to be issued the occupation ribbon + if I get it I really will look like a hero . . . all I have now is the E.T.O. with 1 Battle Star + in Dec. I will get the good Conduct . . . before you know it they will have me all decorated.

The only trouble is time is going so slow the 15th I will has (have) been overseas only 4 months + it seems like 4 years.

Wrote 4 letters yesterday getting pretty good. One to you Janet + both Grandmas

I guess that is enough for now so I will sign off + when you are sending a package sometime send me some more noxzima + don't forget 1 bottle of Vaseline hair tonic want to start to get all darled up you cant tell when I might get home.

In July and August of 1945, the US military implemented a policy to publicly communicate the status of war activities in Japan as soon as possible. It was important for the war effort to airdrop pamphlets and to transmit radio messages to the citizens of Japan, and to share those messages with the rest of the world. The war in Japan became a very important subject of discussion among Bob and his buddies.

On August 6th, the *Enola Gay* dropped a single atomic bomb on the island of Hiroshima, effectively destroying the city and the 2nd Japanese Army.

By August 9th, five million leaflets were dropped by the United States military over major Japanese cities announcing the bombing. The US Office of War Information (OWI) coordinated this activity and transmitted radio messages to the Japanese population every fifteen minutes.

Bob and his buddies were not aware that, on August 9th— the day Bob wrote the letter on the previous page—Japan's senior political ministry engaged in a heated debate concerning their immediate future. Should they continue to fight or surrender? After listening to arguments on both sides, on August 10 the Japanese Emperor finally directed the military to surrender.

The OWI now faced its biggest challenge: to prevent any further civilian or military loss of life, the news regarding Japan's surrender needed to be widely communicated in the Pacific area of operations. Within twenty-four hours, the OWI produced and dropped five million leaflets from American planes over Japan. The message read:

"These American planes are not dropping bombs on you today. American planes are dropping these leaflets instead because the Japanese Government has offered to surrender, and every Japanese has a right to know the terms of that offer and the reply made to it by the United States Government on behalf of itself, the British, the Chinese, and the Russians. Your government now has a chance to end the war immediately. You will see how the war can be ended by reading the two following official statements."

The two paragraphs that followed provided the Japanese surrender, verbatim, and added that the Allies were willing to accept the surrender. Thus, the Japanese people learned for the first time of their governments surrender.

August 11 Germany . . .

Last night as I was on guard they start saying the war is over or will be over by Sunday so the C.O. got 200 qts of wine + 10 barrels of beer + I don't think the party is over just yet + it's 1 o'clock in the afternoon. We shall really find out tonight in the Stars + Stripes. I hope it is true. If it is I'll probably be stuck here for a year or two but it will be worth it if the war is really over.

Didn't receive any mail yesterday. The whole company only got about 20 letters.

Like when you pull 2 hrs guard last night you get the next day off so I'm off today but it don't make any difference because the whole company isn't doing a thing. Except a couple of fellows are fixing up a place for a movies + we are suppose to see one this afternoon with Jack Benny + Alexis Smith its probably about a couple of years old.

My old watch seems to keep perfect time + this pen writes as good as any I've seen.

I guess I will sign off + I hope the war is really over. . . .

August 11 Germany (To Miss Ruth Glover)

Well we just heard that they have signed the papers + the war is officially over. I hope so.

Just seen a traveling movies "The Horn Blows at Midnight" with Jack Benny . . . is guess it is 4 or 5 years old . . . I guess Carl will still be drafted even if the war is over but that will be good because I will be looking for some guy like him so I can come home.

Its pretty rough but if he gets into the Army he will learn how to drink + play cards + how to get out of doing something. That's about all this place time drafting will be.

About 20 low point boys left this morning suppose to join the 104th Div. in Calif. So you cant tell maybe one of these days I'll get home

They are getting a lot of 85 pointers + about in this outfit so when they come home in Nov. the Div. is suppose to be made up of them.

We are about 25 miles from Mannheim so we are going to try to get a pass + go to there tomorrow + look the joint over.

Will sign off now + hope to be home soon.

Bob, Carl, and millions of other members of the armed services were concerned that the end of the war could result in a drop in overall spending, causing a resurgence of the Great Depression.

What they didn't yet know is that there was a significant consumer demand pent up that would fuel strong economic growth. For sure, there would be periods of recession, but increased consumer demand for new cars, new housing, and an increase in the birth rate would propel the US gross national product from $200 million in 1940 to $300 million in 1950. Americans would demand more products and services than ever before.

Unfortunately, an industry that would not do well in the post-war economy was agriculture. Productivity gains in farming led to agricultural overproduction, and farming transitioned into big business. Small family farms could no longer compete with the large, well-resourced farms, so farmers continued to leave for better opportunities. This was evidenced by the drop in the number of farm employees: in 1947, 7.9 million people were employed on farms; this number would drop by half over the next fifty years.

August 12 Sunday Germany

Well we found out last night that the war isn't quite over but the way it sounds it wont last long . . .

They had a big discussion on how they should discharge after the war.

About half the men in this outfit are married+ have children + they figure they should get out just as quick as the high point single men.

We are now eating off of plates + have 6 Germans cleaning up in the mess hall so I guess we will learn to live again.

August 13

Weither Germany

I didn't receive any mail for a couple of days but today I got 4. You, Butch, Janet and Jean.

You asked if I think I'll stay over here well if I get caught over here when the war is finished I think it will be a year or 2 before I get home.

We don't know if the war is over or not.

They haven't got but about 100 fellows left in the company + pretty near every day they ship some out. I don't know what they are going to do.

They shipped some today to a labor Bn.

That's a pretty deal because all you do is guard P.W. + the rest of the time is yours.

I don't know where Arthur is located any more + I wrote to Guadagno + I never got any answer.

I got a letter yesterday from that boy who was suppose to come see you + he is still in Camp Lucky Strike near LeHavre so he hasn't started home yet. He is one of those real religious but a swell guy.

You say to ask for something well we have got 5 packs of cigarettes for 2 weeks so if you can find some send me some.

"Send me some cigarettes: that's for the old duck in the post office".

I think after the war when all these n—rs [Editor's note: the actual word has been censored] *get home we shall have a lot of trouble with them. Over here the people treat them like kings. You can see them anywhere with a white girl. Maybe they will all come back here.*

Write a letter to the old geeser we have in Congress + ask him how long will it take to get the boys home after the war is finished.

Bob's perception of blacks was largely based on his experiences with migrant farm workers in Cutchogue. Often, these workers were poor and uneducated, and they traveled in search of temporary farm work. His comments above are in sharp contrast to the way in which he spoke about his black friends in Cutchogue. He often spoke fondly about Pearl and Annabelle Giles, his childhood neighbors and friends; there was never a hint that he was racially biased.

Before WWII, black immigrants in Germany were called Afrodeutsche, and included thousands of French Senegalese soldiers who remained in Germany following the end of the First World War. Until the Nazi regime took power, black musicians and entertainers were very popular in Germany, especially jazz artists. Two examples of this were the American writer and civil rights activist W.E.B. du Bois and the suffragist Mary Church Terrell, who both attended the University of Berlin. They wrote that there seemed to be less discrimination in Germany than they had experienced in the US. Blacks were also well accepted in German-produced films and had roles in several famous movies. This attitude ended when the Nazis came to power in 1932. Nazi racial purity laws targeted gypsies (called Roma), homosexuals, the mentally challenged, and blacks. Similar to the other groups on this list, thousands of blacks were sent to concentration camps during the war.

August 14 (return address on envelope marked "Guess who")

Well they claim there is some underground going on here so that gives us some more work because they have a few oil wells around here that all that get out of them is road oil + if anybody wanted to blow them up they wouldn't do a heck of a lot.

I guess the war is officially over with what they say. I hope it is anyway.

That chocolate candy gets here O.K.

If you cant find any cigarettes forget about it. I can get along without them.

Sorry to hear you aren't feeling good. It's a funny thing but I haven't felt bad since I've been overseas.

I was talking to one of the medics + he said when you live in tents you don't live so close together so you don't get sick so easy.

I will sign off with lots of love

Prior to WWII, German industry had begun researching the development of synthetic fuels. Hitler planned to make Germany independent of imported oil, and supported many synthetic development efforts. It is estimated that shortly before the start of the war, the Germans had only inventoried approximately fifteen million barrels of fuel—clearly insufficient to support plans for global domination. Increasing the oil supply became a strategic necessity for Germany; in 1939, they signed a peace treaty with Russia, which provided an additional four million barrels of fuel per year. Still more oil was imported from Romania, and by 1941, net imports of oil totaled thirteen million barrels. The Germans were able to increase domestic production of oil over several years from 3.8 million barrels in 1938) to twelve million barrels in 1940. To further add to the inventory, about five million barrels of fuel were seized throughout Europe in 1940.

Prior to invading, Germany had been purchasing oil from Romania. *LIFE* magazine dated February 19, 1940, included a picture of Romanian oil being loaded into tank cars, with the caption: "Oil for Germany moves in these tank cars of American Essolube and British Shell out of Creditui Minier yards near Ploesti (Rumania)." The photo was taken in 1940, after Germany had already invaded Austria and Poland; yet American and British oil companies continued to provide Germany with oil (hence, the Essolube and Shell tank cars).

The Russian-based oil fields also provided an attractive strategic objective; deemed a valuable prize, they gave Hitler another reason to attack Russia.

Despite their aggression and Research and Development efforts, Germany was not able to solve their petroleum deficit. Additionally, Allied bombers targeted German oil fields and production facilities, successfully depleting the German fuel inventories.

Albert Speer, Minister of Armaments and War Production, described the challenges in June 1944: ". . . the Allies staged a new series of attacks which put many fuel plants out of action. On June 22, nine-tenths of the production of airplane fuel was knocked out." In July of 1944, Speer sent a memorandum to Hitler. "I implored Hitler . . . to reserve a significantly larger part of the fighter plane production . . . to protecting the home hydrogenation plants . . ." and on November 10, 1944. "Meanwhile the army, too, had become virtually immobile because of the fuel shortage."

August 15

It's half past ten in the morning . . .

I have today off after guarding the oil wells for 8 hrs. last night

The war is suppose to be definitely over now.

I read where the navy has stopped work on 85 ships already so I hope Daddy don't get laid off.

We are suppose to have another big party tonight.

The way it looks now is the same as before. If I stay in this Division I will be home for Christmas in Nov.

Today is my anniversary 4 months ago today we sailed from New York.

That was a pretty sad day we come down from Camp Shanks in a train + got off opposite 34ᵗʰ St. + then they jammed us on a ferry + took us to Staten Island + as they called our name we climbed up the gangplank + went +got ourselves a bunk + then we sailed off, hit Le Havre two weeks later after a day in Weymouth England. That night we crossed the channel from Eng. To LeHavre they had a fight with a couple of subs. I don't believe I was any (more) scared in my life.

. . . if you haven't sent that package yet throw a comb in it

lots of love.

Bob's reference to the Navy ceasing work on eighty-five ships indicates his concern for his father's job, as well as the thousands of other people employed at the Navy Yard. The US

110

Navy Yard, often referred to as the Brooklyn Navy Yard had an almost two hundred-year-long history of providing significant employment for New York-area residents.

Originally, in the 1700s the Brooklyn waterfront was used for the manufacture of merchant ships. In 1801, The United States Government bought forty acres of docks for $40,000 and the area became an active naval shipyard in 1806. Several famous ships were built in the early days of the shipyard, including Robert Fulton's steamboat the *Fulton*; the *Monitor*, the first ironclad ship, was fitted there with its iron cladding; and the infamous *Maine* was launched from the naval yard in 1890.

During World War II, the yard had four large dry docks five miles of paved streets, barracks, a railroad, foundries warehouses, and shops. It covered over two hundred acres. In 1938 it employed approximately ten thousand people—one third of which were Works Progress Administration (WPA) workers.

The Navy Yard produced several ships of note during WWII; the battleships *Iowa* and *Missouri* were completed in 1942, and President John F. Kennedy's boat, the *PT-109*, was refitted there. At the height of production, over seventy thousand people were employed at the US Navy Yard.

∞∞∞ ∞∞∞ ∞∞∞

Bob had good reason to be concerned about U-boats. In December 1944, the 15th US Army group—consisting of 208 officers and 624 enlisted men, plus an additional 652 men, and the British crew— boarded a British landing ship, the *Empire Javelin*, to cross the English Channel. On 28 December 1944, as the ship was crossing the Channel, it was struck by a torpedo fired by the German submarine U-772. Fortunately, the French ship, *L'Escarmouche*, and other smaller vessels immediately came to the rescue. *L'Escarmouche* came alongside the *Empire Javelin*, enabling many soldiers to jump from its deck to safety aboard

111

L'Escarmouche. Other men were pulled from life rafts, a lifeboat, and some from the sea itself. Only minutes after the first torpedo struck, a second explosion was felt, and at 5:25 p.m., the *Empire Javelin* sank. Thirteen men were missing in action and twenty men were injured during the U-boat attack.

August 17- V. J.

Well today is official V.J. Day

Some of these guys been in the Army a heck of a long time but today was the first day they ever got breakfast in bed.

Now that it's all over I wonder how long I will be stuck here for.

They said the Duration +6 months but they can call anything the duration.

Well we are scheduled to come home next month so we shall see if I stay in outfit

They have more kids here who are about 8-12 than I have ever seen.

I have been trying to get you a cross which the mother got for having a baby, they get a blue one for a boy+ a red one for a girl.

That's about all I can think of to write. Keep your fingers crossed that I come home.

SEPTEMBER 1945—(SCHWABISCH) HALL

Sept. 7 Hall Germany

This will be one of these letters you will get while I am out of airmail stamps.

Now this Division has been alerted for shipment to the states + only going to take guys with 60 points. So it means that I will be transferring again one of these days.

I have been in this outfit pretty near two weeks + haven't got any letters from you although I have received 2 packages + a letter from Grama Glover.

We are living o.k. here now + eating pretty near anything we want.

I am the assistant driver on a 2 ½ ton truck which we haul rations on + I was going to try to get a truck of my own but now they have froze all the ratings in the outfit so I don't think I'll bother. They make truck drivers T/5 that is like this (sketch of a T with 2 chevrons on top) that is 2 stripes with a T underneath it. I will try again when I get to my new outfit.

I hope that everything home is o.k.

I am feeling fine + I think I am gaining weight.

We go about 50 miles everyday one way + 75 every other day to get rations + one day I seen Arthur Sarno walking on the road but we were "high balling" it along so we didn't stop. I think he is in an engineer outfit.

I got 20 points now so I don't expect to be home very soon. They figure every man will be overseas 1 yr to 18 months. The 15th of this month I will have only 5 months in.

Will sign off hoping you get this within a month.

To date, Bob had earned only one quarter of the points needed to be considered eligible to return to the United States. His time served, plus overseas service time, and his battle stars only added up to twenty points—nowhere close to the required eighty-five points.

Bob's unit was now assigned to the town of Hall; originally named Schwäbisch Hall, it had been a strategic area for the Germans during the war. In 1938, the Hessental air base was constructed, and in 1944, a concentration camp was installed near the railway station. The United States Army liberated the concentration camp in 1945.

Sept. 9 Hall, Germany

Well today is sunday + I have got the day off so I thought I might as well write you a letter even though I know you probably wont get it for a month.

I got to thinking last night after reading in the Stars+ Stripes that the Army of Occupation would be up to 45 + me with my 20 it would mean another year over here at least.

What I want to know is if they are drafting anymore guys? There was only one more shipment of guys over here after I got over.

I like this ration job that I am doing now because it is like a civilian job. You go + get it done + then come home.

It's a seven day a week job + you get a day off once in a while.

I will sign off hoping to get some stamps from you

In 1942, the new three-cent "Win the War" US postage stamp became very popular, mostly due to the widespread feeling of patriotism in the country. This successful stamp was followed by the issuance of other new stamps in 1943 and 1944 depicting the flags of European countries. These new stamps were priced at five cents each and were intended for use on V-mail letters to be sent to military personnel stationed overseas.

Soldiers stationed overseas did not have to pay postage to send V-mail letters home. All Bob, or any other serviceman, had to do was write "Free" on the envelope and the Post Office would deliver it. However, it was not uncommon for both the soldier and his family to include an additional five- or six-cent stamp to the regular or waived postage; adding the "paid" stamp was believed to ensure the delivery of the letter.

The mention of time served in the previous letter refers to October 1940 and the beginning of the draft process. President Roosevelt nearly caused a riot among active members of the military service when he asked Congress to lengthen the original twelve-month term of service. Many soldiers were furious upon hearing this, and some even threatened to revolt; however, following the Japanese attack on Pearl Harbor, thousands of men and women proactively volunteered for service. In total, during the 1940 to 1947 period, over ten million men were inducted into the service.

Sept. 14

Just received your letter dated Sept. 6 . . .

As far as Arthur being home in Nov. I think that is a lot of bolongie because last night the headlines were the men with 2 yrs of service would be out in a yr. He is in the same Division as I am only in the Engineers attached to this Division + I'm in the 33rd Armed Regt. He must have thought he was gone home with the 106th.

This job what I am doing is o.k. you get 1 day off a week + we are only working from 1-6 in the afternoon.

It's hard to write a letter because everything is about the same.

The other night the(y) broke up a Hitlers Youth meeting here +

> *what they did to those kids you can put on paper. It wasn't that bad but they shure beat the hell out of them.*
>
> *Don't forget to send stamps + hair tonic. I didn't get paid last month so I cant buy any.*
>
> *I am sending a patch for Janet + I will sign off love to all*

The Hitler Youth Movement was designed to capture the hearts and minds of German children. To create a more perfect nation, Hitler wanted the German youth to be healthy and well educated.

The Hitler Youth (Hitlerjugend) was designed for teenage boys, it prepared them for military service. In 1936, an estimated four million children belonged to the organization.

The organization lasted almost thirty-three years, from 1922 to 1945. Many future leaders of East and West Germany were former members of the organization; Pope Benedict XVI admitted publicly that he had been a member. Following the end of the war, the Allies disbanded the Hitler Youth, and no efforts were made to prosecute any war crimes allegedly committed by these children.

> *Sept 18, Hall, Germany . . .*
>
> *The only reason I thought about signing up is you get some good breaks but I don't believe it is worth it.*
>
> *What's the name of the town where Shiller's statue is? Weimar + is it in the North or South or where (?) . . . Stuttgart . . . I have been through it a couple of times+ went for a week to the out skirts to get rations*
>
> *Gets pretty hot over here in the day time*
>
> *Still eating like Kings but I hear we are going to ship out.*
>
> *Sure was glad to here from you + I will get home some day.*

Bob's mother, Louise, insisted that her family were descendants of the famous German poet Friedrich Schiller. She cited as evidence the fact that several of her family members were listed as relatives of Schiller in a book published in Germany. Apparently, in Germany, it was an honor to claim a kinship with the famous poet, as the book listed many, many relatives.

JCF Schiller (Johann Christoph Friedrich Schiller, 1759-1805) was known for his most famous musical poem "Ode to Joy" as the final part of Beethoven's Ninth Symphony. Schiller was a writer, historian, philosopher, and studied both law and medicine.

Bob was simply humoring his mother by mentioning Schiller in his letter.

Sept 19, Wed, Hall

Well Saturday I ship out of this Division to the 1st Armored Div. it is rumored. So maybe you had better slip a $5 money order in the next letter because, you see, you sign the payroll on the 15th + get paid the last day of the month + if you ship from one outfit to another you just miss that month's pay. It's a sad story, isn't it?

Received 4 old letters today from you + 1 from Janet dated around the last of August. Some were written while you were at Greenport.

Well the way it looks as things are shaping up the Critical score will wind up at 45 so I now have officially 20 it will be another Year at 2 points per month if I stay here + 2 years if I come to the states. I think it would be better to sweat out another year over here. You know the Army isn't so bad if you get situated right + get to know the right people. This time as you know I got in the ration section+ you have a lot of influence with all that food.

You say you read my letters over + over. It is probably because you cant understand them the first time.

There isn't nothing special I want for Christmas except send me a

---

quart or pint of good wisky.

Don't think I'm beginning to be a rummy or anything I don't like it any better than I ever did. Only thing is I thought it would be nice for my second Christmas away from home.

These Germans are starting to act up a little bit but I guess it will be O.K.

I was thinking that I have had my watch for a year now + for the $15 it cost + the $9 to get it fixed it is O.K.

PS: did you ever send the hair tonic

Sept 20, Thurs, Hall

. . . you said something about me coming home well let's stop kidding I wont be home for a yr. or more but don't worry about that because nobody is working hard here now.

Saturday I ship out to the 13th tank Bn. (Battalion?). I think it is in the 1st Armored Division around Frankfort, about 160 miles, but I was down around there once so it wont be anything new.

I don't believe I will ever get another place as easy as I've had it here for the last month.

I sure appreciate you sending the cigarettes because I can use them.

Another thing that hurts about shipping out is there were only 15 guys in the section + we all got to be pretty good friends.

The hardest thing it have keeping is a comb so maybe you can send one or 2 with one of the packages. Don't forget to send me about 5 dollars money order + some Hair oil.

Sept 24

Well I've finally got settled again + this time it is in the 1st Armored + we pretty near got back to Coblenz only 66 km. from it. Come about 160 miles I guess come through Frankfort +Hidelburg but we wind up practically sitting on the Rhine in a little town south + I guess of Wiesbaden + it is a pretty city.

Today I drove a officer to Damstadt + left him there + come back about 120 miles round trip. I'd like to get a steady job driving but they made me a Scout in the Reconniance platoon.

I guess I'll be here a while so you can write plenty of mail.

I pretty near had a nervous breakdown yesterday when one of the fellows told me all under 45 points will stay for 3 yrs.

In one year over here I think a fellow will be walking on his hands Hieling Hitler . . .

Hq. Co. 13th Tank Bn.

A.P.O. 251 c/o Postmaster

It don't look like I'll get paid this month but the French are across the River + they will give $3-$4 a pack for cigarettes

Sept 25, Tuesday

We didn't do much except clean up halftracks today because there is a big inspection coming up next Tuesday by the 7th Army.

I have a good chance to buy a pistol if I ever get paid for $10 + if I still can get it I will. The way some of these Germans are fooling around I think it's a good thing to have.

The main topic of conversation over here is when will we get home? If they would set up a definite time that you have to stay over here you would at least feel better.

Did they ever pass that compulsory draft law? I can see those 5 yrs that the 1st World War vets stayed here.

Enough crying here but it sure does make me mad to think about it.

In that city I was talking about (Wiesbaden) they have the most beautiful Red Cross Club I have ever seen. It must have cost at least a couple of million, it takes up a whole block + there is Coke+ Donut Room, Lemonade +Donut Room, + the coffee + donut room + they have these Germans dressed up in a white coat + Black pants.

Wiesbaden + Hidleburg are the prettiest German cities I've seen. The flattest one I've seen is Aachen but there is plenty of smaller towns that are "Allus Kaput".

If they keep me over here, I expect to see Berlin one of these days.

How are the kids making out in school? + is the navy yard still perculating + when is Carl going to be drafted now that the war is over

I haven't got any feelings for these young guys + these guys who have been exempt, they cant be essential anymore + I cant understand why they are discharging guys in the states regardless of points + they didn't have to be overseas. There was only one more shipment of guys that came across after me.

I know that it isn't my turn to come home yet but one of these days it will come + I don't want to have to stay here because they haven't got any replacements over here.

Had a pass to Paris offered to me this morning but I couldn't go because I didn't have any money but it is just as good because those French aren't any good.

I don't believe I've ever been cold so long as I've been here 3 days + it was pretty warm where we come from + it's right on the Rhine here + I cant get enough clothes on. I sleep with my long

> *underwear on + in the sleeping bag with 2 blankets over me + I just about keep warm.*
>
> *Well I will sign off now with lots of love. I hope you are all well + at least warm.*

Donuts were a warm and tasty snack that reminded servicemen of home; plus, for the soldiers, the donuts came with the added treat of getting to personally interact with the Red Cross women who provided them.

Bob asked about Carl's status, because men were still being drafted into the service despite the end of the war. The Selective Service Act made men between ages eighteen and forty-five eligible for military service and required all men between ages eighteen and sixty-five to register. The end point of service was extended to six months after the war. This policy lasted until the end of 1947 when the wartime Selective Service Act expired. Following several extensions of the act by Congress, over ten million men had been inducted.

Bob visited the Wiesbaden Red Cross Club; these recreational clubs offered many types of entertainment for soldiers, including music, golf, and card games. Hotels such as the Kurhaus, Neroberg, Opelbad, Palast (headquarters of the Military Government), Schwarzer Bock, and Goldener Brunnen were all locations where servicemen could spend time off duty.

The Kurhaus had the famous "Eagle Club," which was operated by the American Red Cross and was where international celebrities like Frank Sinatra and Bob Hope entertained the troops.

∞∞ ∞∞ ∞∞

The Army knew that Bob wasn't alone in his attitude toward the French. One million copies of the Army guide *A Pocket*

Guide To France, later renamed *Instructions for American Servicemen in France during World War II*, were requested by the War Department in a top-secret message and provided to servicemen in 1944. The book was intended "to give a general idea of the country concerned, to serve as a guide to behavior in relation to the civil population, and to contain a suitable, concise vocabulary." It was originally a classified book intended to give Allied soldiers a sense of the country they would soon overrun.

The US soldiers' dispassionate attitude toward the French began in 1940; France had just signed a peace treaty with the invading Germans, and in 1942, the first enemies American troops encountered in Morocco and Algeria during the North African invasion were French soldiers and sailors.

"We are friends of the French and they are friends of ours," the guide instructs. "The Germans are our enemies and we are theirs." The liberators were told to expect "a big welcome from the French. Americans are popular in France."

The guide stereotyped France's culture and people. The French were said to be "mentally quick," "economical," "realistic," and "individualists." They are "good talkers and magnificent cooks," but "they have little curiosity." Residents of Marseilles "are southern, turbulent and hot-headed." The guide also asserted, "Respect for work is a profound principle in France."

GIs who wanted to marry a French bride and bring her to the US were cautioned that "there will be no government transportation available for a wife."

Following four years of military occupation, and knowing that two million Frenchmen were held in Germany as POWs, the guide advised: "The French may not be able to be proud of how things look now so don't rub it in."

Bob had likely formed his opinion of the French largely based on what he had heard from his fellow soldiers, and not much else.

Sept 26, Wed.

It's only noon hr. but I thought I would start the letter. This morning we got in the halftrack + started + went about 60 miles giving it a road test.

The fellows were telling me that this was in the Stars + Stripes + over the radio that you will only have to stay here in occupation for 6 months + it was suppose to begin Sept. 1st. I should wind up in Feb + get home in about July.

When I was in the 106th + expected to go to the Pacific we had a saying "Golden Gate in 48 bread line in 49". I think I will beat that schedule.

So how is everything home? I suppose everything is the same.

The summer went fast + before I know it, it will be snowing here

The 3rd Inf. Regiment is about 20 miles from here so maybe someday I'll go over there + see if I can see any of the old boys who stayed there.

Now I don't know anybody here. Before I was always with some guys that I kind of knew in the states

It don't pay to make friends in the army because in 2 or 3 weeks you leave them.

I think I'll start getting mail from you about Sunday.

PS Your no. 1 Son 42161467

HDq. Co. 13 Tank BN. A.P.O. 251

c/o Butcher of mail N.Y.C.

Sept 28

. . . did I tell you about these 45 day furloughs they are starting to the states+ they give them to the guys with the least number of points so I must be down in there someplace.

I'm on guard tonight + tomorrow so I'll have plenty of time to lay around. The way they work that is you are on 2 + off 4 for 24 hrs. so that isn't so bad . . .

They just come around asking for 2 guys to go on pass to Switzerland + 1 to England, probably when I get paid they will freeze all passes or something.

I've seen some of the watches that guys have bought in Switzerland + they are o.k.

It will be pretty good to see New York again.

I've made a decision that I will go back to work within the first week I am home.

They say it isn't good to lay around to long when you get out

PS: Them stamps had better get on the ball.

OCTOBER 1945—DISPLACED PERSONS

Oct 2

No mail yet nobody is getting any they claim it's on account of the strike.

I received another package which says do not open till Christmas, that makes 3 I've got.

I put in for a $55 money order, probably get it tomorrow.

There isn't anything new.

Except this Division is suppose to come home in June so I guess I ought to be ready then.

I wish there was something to write about.

They have started shifting guys around again for redeployment since the strike is over.

The 3ʳᵈ Armd. moved out of here today so the old ration gang left.

Have two good buddies now one is from Jersey + the other from Kentucky we go all over together

The guy from Jersey is "Whittie" he's about 5 ft. 6 + real thin the guy from Kentucky is "slim" he's about an inch shorter than me with black wavy hair. We get a long good. "Whittie" is always cracking a Joke + Slim is solemn as they come . . . laughs once in a while.

I'm just writing this stuff so there will be something to write about.

I remember 1 yr. ago yesterday I got my notice for induction. We were working on an A.K.A. I think 62. I didn't think I would be around this yr. at this time.

Saturday (tomorrow) all the fellows who signed up for more time

> *in the army start home for their furlough. We all give them a razzen about 3 yrs in Japan + 3 yrs in Duechland but the more signs up the merrier for me.*
>
> *There is always time to sign up again when you get discharged*
>
> *Hope you can get a camera. Take the money I am sending home + pay for it.*
>
> *Was offered $50 for the gun I paid $40 for today. Everybody is going gun crazy here since some of these stories they are putting out.*

Bob had worked on several Attack Cargo Ships (designated AKA) as an employee at the Navy Yard; these were US Navy ships that carried troops, equipment, and supplies and specialized in naval gunfire during amphibious assaults. More than one hundred of these ships were built during World War II.

The versatile AKA ships, used mostly in the Pacific, were able to perform many functions. They carried landing craft vehicles and at the same time utilized Combat Information Centers using radio communications.

Bob refers to the number sixty-two, which is likely a reference to the USS *Sheliak* (AKA-62), an attack cargo ship manned by the Coast Guard. It served for seventeen months during WWII.

Bob received his Christmas presents early; his family wanted to be proactive and beat the postal "traffic jam" that was sure to come during the holiday season. Cross-Atlantic cargo space for US Mail became increasingly limited as more and more soldiers, sailors, and equipment were sent to and from Europe.

Oct. 2

Well I received another package with the cigarettes in it from you + Grama Macomber. I also got 2 letters from you + 1 from Dolly.

Tell daddy not to worry about me signing up for any more time. There for a while I thought I would for the 45 days home but now they are giving the occupation troop(s) 45 day rotation furloughs so maybe I'll be lucky enough to get one.

I haven't got paid in 2 months now so I'm pretty short on cash. In fact I am "bustakated"[1]

How are the bonds coming in?

Thanks for paying the insurance

I might live the next 17 years to collect that thousand.

Why in Hell don't Carl think they'll take him? He ought to make out damn good with these Dutchmen. Let them grab all those guys home + shove them in the army.

There must be a lot of these guys who were essential to the war effort but they cant be any more. In about 6 mo when I get ready to leave this Superland I want replacements + there is a lot of guys over here yet with children who should be home.

Between now + the 15th of this month we are suppose to move to another town or city about 200 miles it's named Ulm.

I tried to look up Guadagno but his company is about 50 miles from here.

It gets dark here now about 6:30 + we start to fool with our thumbs.

---

[1] **Definition**: bus·ti·cat·ed, *Northern US.* To break into pieces.

We are in a town about the size of Peconic not even as big as Cutchogue.

The 15th of this mo I will have been overseas 6 mo. It don't sound very long does it but that is a half a yr + before you know it it will be another 6 mo + that's when I will quit.

I got hold of a Life magazine over here + I see where everybody was celebrating the end of the war.

It looks funny as hell.

All anybody did over here was say yeh.

I think I got a hole in my front tooth in the back so I suppose I shall have to go + fight with another dentist.

They had a reprint in the Stars+ Stripes where some New York Times writer wrote where the boys over here think more of the Germans than some of our allies. Well I think more of them than the French just on what some of the boys told me who were in France+ if he don't like it let him come over here instead of sitting behind some desk + drinking Ice Cream sodas.

I don't think much of any of these people. None of them are like Americans. They just haven't got the brains.

Today I was over the Kitchen + I got to talking to one of the cooks about fighting + so on so he called one of the Germans over that work in the kitchen + I see the Gerrie was pretty big so I kinda backed out till the German called me yellow so then I clipped him a couple of times just to show him that Americans are still around.

You see plenty of the Germans going home + you also see plenty with a leg or an arm going . . .

Oct 4 Thursday

Tomorrow I am going to LeHavre but don't get all excited I aint coming home. There are 16 of us going there to bring trucks + Jeeps back here. It is going to take a week so don't expect any mail for a week. They say it is about 700 miles 1 way but I don't think it's that far. At least I will see France again + it will kill a week's time.

When a G.I. goes to France he is suppose to collect $18.75 so I cant lose on the money angle.

Don't forget no mail for a week that don't mean you cant write.

Have been waiting very patiently for some stamps but none as yet.

Yesterday I received 5 letters 2 from you 1 a piece from Gram, Joan + Carl.

Where the heck do some of these people get the idea we are having a good time over here.

Seen the picture God is my Co pilot last night + it was pretty good. First time I went to a show in a long time.

You'll have to explain to my writers that I am out of stamps.

October 11, 1945

As you read along you will find that I made it back from France in one piece. You are probably mad for not getting any mail but I wrote you that I was going but one of the fellows only mailed in 2 or 3 days ago.

We had a nice trip all the way to Camp Lucky Strike over 1100 miles round trip. We stayed at the Metz, Soissons + Lucky Strike overnight 2 nights,1 coming and 1 going at Metz +Soissons

I yelled in the English Channel but I don't suppose you heard me.

> *I collected $17.50 off of the French government, had a good time seen the play Golden Boy + a couple of other stage shows + drove a 2 ½ ton halfway back.*
>
> *Some of the fellows said they heard over the radio that they are going to send over 150,000 replacements from the states.*
>
> *I read in the paper where 2 yr. men will be eligible for discharge in March so that don't look so good for me.*
>
> *Nothing else new hope all of you are o.k. + will write again tomorrow*
>
> *No mail.*

Bob drove to Camp Lucky Strike, a holding area for Recovered Allied Military Personnel (RAMPS), i.e. prisoners of war who had been released. Camp Lucky Strike was one of the processing areas where former POWs were brought in by air from camps across Germany. Many of these RAMPS were destined to be sent home to the United States. Approximately eighty thousand POWs were processed there, some departing by air and some departing by ship from LeHavre.

> *Oct 12 Niederwalluf*
> *No we didn't move I just learned how to spell the name of this town we are in you pronounce it like Need A Wolf.*
> *As you know I just got back from a 6 day trip to LeHavre well tomorrow I am going on a 3 day trip to Holland don't know what for or anything it looks like they have elected me the company long distant man.*
> *Didn't receive any mail from again today. Hope you are O.K.*
> *Don't forget you wont get any mail for 3 more days.*
> *You know I am kind of feeling old+ discussed + don't give a damn All the sergeants have a rough time getting me out. But everything is O.K.*

> Write soon I am sort of worrying because there has been no mail in a week.
> In case you have lost the address it is
> PS Your no. 1 Son 42161467
> HDq. Co. 13 Tank BN. A.P.O. 251
> c/o Postmaster N.Y. N. Y.

> October 15 or 16 Tuesday
>
> . . . You asked if we got a shoulder patch every time we change well every different division you go to you get a different patch now I have the same as before only instead of a 3 it has got a I in it.
>
> Got your stamps thanks a lot.
>
> Don't worry I wont open the package before Christmas it is stated so on the box.
>
> When I went to the 33rd I started figuring how to get something easy + I got it. I am working on a couple of angles here. There are to many easy jobs in this army to work hard. All you got to do is to know the right people +that takes a few weeks. But I figure in a week or two it will be time to start asking questions.
>
> What is the matter with these longshoremen, they had plenty of guys in France to come home but now they are starting to ship them back to Germany + as for those British I think we should take the Queens + keep them for the money they owe us.
>
> Only went about 40 miles into Holland but what I see was nice seen a couple of these canals where the water is way over sea level. I don't remember if I told you yesterday but we went along the Rhine.

Bob was growing more aware of economics and politics and their global world. Specifically, he commented on the ability of the United Kingdom to repay the United States for expenses incurred during World War II, and on the Wildcat Strike taking place in New York. The strike came when the International Longshoremen's Association attempted to negotiate weight limits on loads coming off ships. On October 1, 1945, the negotiations stalled and thirty-five thousand longshoremen conducted a "wildcat" strike at Chelsea Piers in NYC. The strike lasted almost a month, and resulted in some improvements in working conditions, but no change in weight limits.

In 1941, the United States, officially a neutral nation at the time, offered to provide war materials and lend capital to countries who were fighting Germany. Britain in particular needed funds for food and reconstruction. In 1945, the United States loaned the United Kingdom a significant amount of money: $4.33 billion (£2.2 billion) to Britain, at a rate of two percent annual interest.

Bob had little reason to be concerned regarding repayment; over a fifty-year period, the United Kingdom paid back a total of $7.5 billion (£3.8 billion), including interest, to the United States.

Undated letter sent in Oct 17 postmarked envelope

Just got back from Holland + I still haven't gotten any mail it been about 10 days since I got mail . . .

Had a nice trip to Holland took 5 truck loads of Belgium + Holland D.P. (Displaced persons) home. Took the Belgiums to Liege + the Dutch to Maastrich Holland. Didn't get there till about 2 o'clock Sunday morning so we slept there + about 8 o'clock Sunday morning we left and went back through Verviers, Namur +Liege trying to find some place to stay for Sunday + Eat but there wasn't any place, so we head for Aachen + we get there + go eat at an English place + had tea + a fish cake I think, so we decide we don't like this place + the Limies tell us there is an American transit camp at Cologne so we go there + get there o.k.

> + eat supper at a limie place + have cabbage with a piece of mutton with tea but it tasted pretty good. So then we look for the American Place + no such thing in Cologne so we take off down the road + slept in the trucks. This morning we pulled into Wiesbaden about 10 oclock took a shower + went to the Red Cross has donuts + coffee + I just got home.
>
> Well I guess that is the story . . .

Bob and his buddies helped many Belgian and Dutch POWs to return to their homelands after being held in Germany.

Hundreds of Belgians and Dutch formed "resistance" organizations during WWII; their roles were largely to help guide Allied aircraft and to provide safe passage for Allied servicemen as they crossed through the area.

Two hundred Belgians and Dutch resistance volunteers created secret Service EVA (Evasion) escape lines, and assisted the Allies in many ways. They guided airmen and ground troops, provided shelter, made false IDs, transported messages, and offered medical care to Allied soldiers. An estimated two hundred Allied airmen were aided from various Allied countries: the United States, Britain, Canada, and New Zealand. An example of an escape route would begin in Holland, go through Belgium, then across France, over the Pyrenees to Spain, and eventually back to England

The Service EVA took great risks and many members were captured by the Germans. By 1945, it was estimated that the Germans had arrested as many as seventy members; many were transported to Germany, and others are known to have been executed.

> October 18
>
> Received 2 letters last night dated Oct 12+13 so that isn't so bad. Sometimes it comes quick then another time it takes 2 or 3 weeks.

For an average package it takes around 1 month.

I will try + send a money order home this month because I will get 3 months pay. I guess it will be a little over $100. Suppose to get $64 a month but you take out 18.25 bond. That leaves $45.75 then $6.40 insurance, I guess around $120.

I know how that Donald feels but there will be a lot of guys hurting like that but somebody got to come over another 6 mo to 1 yr + I want to get out + there is plenty of other guys here.

Did I tell you about when we took these D.P. to Holland before we left some guy came out + gave each guy 5 packs of marvel cigarettes that's that UN sure these guys are living off of the U.S. Don't give a blessed thing for these people over here they have enough.

What I get a kick out of is the French steal everything they can get off the German. Horses to a car you see it going back to France with the French flag painted all over it.

We are suppose to move very shortly to Hall or near Hall.

I'll be glad to get away from the Rhine maybe I'll be able to see the sun again.

It's Friday afternoon + there isn't nothing to do so maybe I'll see if I can hook a ride to Weisbaden + go to the show.

P.S. Here's a picture of the old boy.

Bob was becoming more interested in post-war politics and was frustrated by what he observed. He perceived that Displaced Persons were, at times, being given unnecessary free goods, like unusually high quantities of cigarettes.

He also referred to the genesis of the United Nations—a widely published event at the time. In 1945, representatives of fifty countries met in San Francisco to prepare the United Nations

Charter. The Charter was signed on June 26, 1945 creating the largest forum in the world for members to express their views and to settle their differences.

October 20

Received your letter + the mirror + a letter from Butch yesterday.

Your letters get here in 4 or 5 days.

Instead of that bottle of whiskey I asked you for Christmas how about sending me a camera + some films it don't have to be a high price one. Just one that will take pictures.

Didn't get the money order yet don't need it now + will send that much more home on payday.

Tell Butch that the next German helmet that I see I will get + I will get one if I have to take one off of a German cop.

Its been foggie + cold the last 3 days + I hope we get out of here next Wednesday.

Seen a good picture yesterday afternoon A Bell for Adano. We, me + another fellow are going to Weisbaden again this afternoon. It isn't very far + you can get ice cream there for a nickel a plate. There are 2 army shows + the red cross I told you about that place. They even have 2 Krout orchestras playing you can get donuts + coffee or lemonade or cokes. The only thing you have to pay for is the cokes.

They hold all these war crimes trials there so there is plenty of Brass around + plenty of wacs.

It is a plenty big town + isn't banged up so much.

Its funny how these people live over here they all live Together in one spot not like the states where you can find farm house or any kind of house all along the roads. Well you will never find a Krout home unless he is so close to his neighbor that there is room only

---

for a wagon.

Read in the Stars + Stripes where all the wacs out of E.T.O. by April

I was figuring up my point score last night + in June I'll have my 35 points + that is going to be the discharge level when they get down there.

I hope all of you are alright.

You were talking about clothes well we still have those long underwear with our O.D.'s + they give us one sweater + I hooked another 2 pr.   of woolen socks rubbers (cant spell goolashes) + an overcoat so I guess I'll be warm enough. If I get cold I always have my 2 blanks + my sleeping bag.

The food is alright but there will never be another place like the 33rd. We are going there + stay for 5 days + then go to Ulm so maybe I'll see some of the guys.

What do you mean I should see Daddy with his glasses?

How about a picture

I was thinking about that old box camera you have at home how about that? If I loose it we wont have lost much.

Oct. 20

This is the second letter for today . . . you said in the letter Oct 2 you sent the 5 dollars the day before. Well I didn't get it yet but it will be coming along

Received your dollar bill O.K. I guess you know we cant spend it here but the French or English will give you from 3-5 dollar for an American dollar. We use this invasion money.

I go on guard again tonight

What do you mean you sent everything I asked for, you said to ask for something well how about a box with some candy + a couple of packs of cigarettes, send what you want to, we are getting better rations now, about 10 pks of cigarettes a week with about 10 candy bar.

There isn't nothing special I want, everything seems to be o.k.

Run into one of my old buddies today in Wiesbaden. From Brooklyn+ he had just broke his nose playing football.

Just got an idea of what you meant when you said hope your Christmas package don't bust. Don't know if I'll be able to get any of you people anything for Christmas.

Oct. 22 . . .

We are suppose to move to Hall Wednesday for ten day or two weeks + then go to Ulm + be M. P.

They don't get mail on Sunday so I didn't get any yesterday.

If we don't do anything this afternoon I'm going to Wiesbaden to take a shower.

Just got back from Wiesbaden the mail hasn't come in yet. Hope I get some. I will finish this when they give out the mail

Just received a package mailed to the 33rd with the Noxema Candy + Socks + Combs. Thanks a lot+ a carton of cigarettes + a wash rag. Again thanks a lot.

Didn't receive any letters I guess they will come tomorrow

We will be pretty busy tomorrow getting ready to move Wednesday so If I don't write you will know everything is o.k.

I tell you what when I get paid I will send some money home + you can get me a camera.

I was looking around in Wiesbaden today for something to buy for all of you for Christmas but these people don't have anything yet. I haven't even seen a Christmas Card.

Glad to hear the strike is over. I mean the longshoremen . . .

P.S. Butch must be pretty good in school.

. . . used all the other tablet up so I have to use this one. I am pretty near out of stationery so you can throw some in a package if you want to. I hope I aint asking you for too many packages.

If I get paid next month I should get 3 months pay so I will send some home.

I think I look pretty sharp sometimes when I get dressed up after+ I get some Hinnie squaw to press my O.D.s + get on my E.T.O. Jacket.

I guess all the guys in the states have them now that is them short jackets with the tight fit.

A great big Irish man named Toughie (you know Roger Toughie the gangster) is suppose to look up daddy in the navy yard, he used to be a blacksmith there + he was going to see if he could get his old job back.

Had a slight cold last week but it is o.k. now.

Don't forget to send some stamps + that $5 I asked for.

You wont get any more mail till I get some cash or some stamps.

Love, Robert

The term "Heinie" was originally British slang for a German person. It probably has its roots in the German name Heinrich.

October 27

Yesterday I got 2 letters + another package from you that says do not open til Christmas.

Still didn't get the $5 money order or the hair tonic.

I didn't realize Dolly was so old.

I read where we are going to get 2 more medals so that makes 4 ribbons I'll have. E.T.O., good conduct, Victory, Post Pearl Harbor + when they get the occupation out it will be 5. I'll look like an old soldier.

Have had pretty nice weather here last couple of days.

We aren't doing anything here

October 29

Received the package with the box of lofts candy in it + a letter with the money order. Thanks a lot.

Wish there was something to write about.

I think we get paid Wednesday + I guess I get a $100 or more so I'm going to buy myself a pistol to many guys are getting hurt around here

They generally pick on a single guy. It's the Polish + the Germans

You have to pay from $25 to $40 for one pistol but it's a lot better than getting a knife in your back.

I have to go on guard in 60 minutes so I'll sign off.

Despite the fact that the war was officially over, great unrest continued in Europe. Bob's comments regarding the Germans and Poles, both groups likely refugees, are not surprising. These were desperate people living in dangerous times.

Since the beginning of the war, life for the German people was very difficult, and the basic necessities of life were often nonexistent. In 1945 the food supply broke down, and even everyday consumables, like water, became questionable for drinking or for use in cooking. The situation deteriorated so badly, that it was rumored some Germans had resorted to cannibalism in order to survive.

Thousands of Germans fled the Russian-occupied East Germany for West Germany, believing they would fare better under United States control. They rushed to West Germany by any means necessary, and the journey was often unsafe. One such example was the practice of overloading ships in the Baltic Sea with fleeing East Germans; the excess weight caused many vessels to capsize and hundreds of people drowned.

Another example of the difficulties faced by German citizens was the inability to regain their personal property. In Poland, farms and other property owned by Germans before the war were being given to Polish citizens. Germans who had been living in Poland for years were expelled from the country; most attempted to return to Germany, but again, found the trip to be a long and dangerous journey.

October 29

This is number 2 letter for today but it is evening now + there isn't nothing doing.

You would be surprised how many guys are signing up for 1 ½ or 3 yrs in this army.

It is very tempting though for a 60 day fourlough. They have hooked 13 guys out of this company already they tell them that story of being home for Christmas well what about next Christmas.

I guess its alright for a single fellow who hasn't got any trade or

---

anything else in civilian live but I don't believe they can hook me.

There is no telling I might be over here longer than 18 months without a fourlough.

When I seen a movie tonight but most of them make me homesick so I try + stay away.

PS started to put my old address on the envelope

What a job to get a money order cashed I think before I can get it cashed I'll have to see a general.

Bob knew that the lack of a high school diploma or any trade certification would be a challenge for him when looking for employment after he left the Army. He began to think about viable options for a career and the education he would need to complete in order to successfully land a suitable job.

NOVEMBER 1945—SOUVENIRS

Nov. 1, 1945

Well I finally got paid again $120.07 that isn't much for 3 months is it. I bought a sweet Mauser 32 pistol for $40. That sounds like a lot of money but its good protection + I can always get my money back. It is suppose to be the best pistol made of it caliber. I paid $10 I owed + going to send $50 home to you + keep $37 in case something happens that I don't get paid again for a couple of months.

I sure am happy with my gun + I hope you aren't mad for me buying it.

Haven't received any mail last couple of days. Hope you all you people are o.k.

They claim according to latest "poop" that all men over here will be out of the E.T. in 9 months that brings me up to about July. Maybe I'll get home for my birthday.

Bob wanted the gun partially as a war souvenir, but also for protection. Looting—by citizens as well as the military—began many months before the highly publicized 3rd Army's pillaging of Hitler's wine cellar in May 1945.

For thousands of GIs stationed in Europe, souvenir hunting became something of a sport and a hobby.

Valuables, including liquor, jewels, and war materials were especially sought after; the fervor was accelerated following an announcement that US soldiers had actually found crown jewels hidden in a simple box in a castle.

US Army policy following the end of the war enabled soldiers to take home virtually any items they could carry or have shipped. It was not unusual for a returning soldier to come home with a duffel bag full of German items. It was estimated that the first five thousand soldiers who returned home from Europe carried over twenty thousand German weapons with them. They took pistols, knives, watches—anything of value that could be perceived as a war prize. This staggering number earned US soldiers the nickname "The Lootwaffe."

Several studies have since examined the reasons for this fervid souvenir hunting, suggesting that soldiers were motivated by four basic issues:

a. Soldiers wanted keepsakes from the war,
b. They also wanted to make a profit,
c. Necessity occasionally played a role; for example, a soldier might actually need a watch.
d. Finally, it was determined that revenge was a motivating factor. Soldiers wanted to "get even" with the Nazis, and did so by taking items.

General Eisenhower issued orders to stop all looting; this presented the Army with the almost impossible task of gaining control over the situation.

Nov. 5 Monday

. . . We moved into better billets[2] today. I guess it was a hotel because every room has a sink + all the rooms are small.

Sent the money order yesterday hope you have it.

Still didn't get mine cashed but I will one of these days.

It feels cold enough to Snow today . . .

---

[2] **Definition:** billets, assigned quarters

Nov 19, Germany

. . . They are out getting some radios off of these Germans so we can have them here.

They work anything like that this way, they go to the Burgermaster + tell him what they want + if he don't get it, the army looks around + if they see the Burgermaster[3] didn't look to hard, they take + slap him in jail.

Like all Breweries + lumber yards + anything else they see like that they slap a sign on it + take it over. But all of the stuff they get is suppose to be legal so they tell the people that they will pay the German government for it + what they do is take it off Germany's war debt to the U.S.

This atomic bomb that they have invented must be quiet a weapon but they had better be careful how they use it.

We heard today that Russia is fighting the Japs hope it is true.

All we are doing is taking it easy, it is too good to last+ everybody is restless so I think something is going to happen

But you cant tell about anything here.

That sure was a good picture dolly sent me.

I guess everything is o.k. home. I see in the Stars + Stripes where they are fixing the Empire State Bldg.

I hope you didn't forget to send the Vaseline Hair Tonic my hair is just about as dry as it can get, send a package.

Love
Guess who?

---

[3] **Definition:** burgermaster, the chief magistrate of a town in Austria, Belgium, Germany, or the Netherlands; mayor.

Germany

Well yesterday the mail started coming again, 6 letters, 3 from you 1 from Janet, Butch+ Gram Macomber. Yours came pretty good Oct 22-24-26. That isn't so bad.

I read in the Stars + Stripes where they are giving packages with "Do Not open till Xmas" preference over the other packages. I guess that is why they come so good. You know I have 3 already. They don't stamp no date on the packages so you don't know how long it takes.

It isn't bad here now we aren't doing nothing. Just pulling guard.

In the morning we go to the Red Cross + have coffee + cake + in the afternoon we generally play ping pong or something

Slim, my buddy, is in Paris after a Jeep for Military Gov., + Whittey is going to England on pass Monday so I'll be all alone till Slim gets back.

I sure would like to see the Pacific fleet.

Nov. 4, Sunday

Received a letter from Dolly + butch yesterday

Enclosed find a money order for $55. Hope you get it o.k.

There isn't nothing new we will be here in Hall till the 15th or 20th according to latest Rumors. Tomorrow we are going to move into better billets here.

Just wrote to get this money order off . . .

Nov. 6 Tuesday

Hall, Germany . . .

Had some trouble last night one of the boys shot up two "hinnies" so they have got him under guard + arrested to quarters. So now we have to turn in all foreign weapons everybody is putting up a big kick but it come from the Bn. Commander so I guess it will have to be done.

Read the clipping they even got the officers worried about Christmas packages.

Well how is Carl making out? You know I didn't have such a bad break I didn't go in the army till 4 months after I registered. Well anyhow the last of this month I will be in a year.

Send package.

Nov. 8 . . .

Have been folding tents this morning to turn in I hope we never have to use them again.

They are taking all G.I. clothing off any civilians that have them. A lot of them bought them off the soldiers but now they have about 20 fellows + that's all they are doing is collecting clothing.

There is a place now where we can get dry cleaning done so that is pretty good.

They have cut out giving furloughs for enlisting for 1 ½ yrs. + only give it for 3 yrs.

I cant understand where the packages are you said (I think you sent 7 carton of cigarette well I only got 3)

Hope you got the money order.

I bet it will be a pretty hard job to go back to work + settle down when I get home.

Nov. 11, Tuesday

Well we got to Heidelberg + at 7th Army Headquarters + it looks like we are going to work out from here. It seems that this Lt. Dearborn is going to inspect outfits before they go home so I guess we'll be riding all over the American Part of Germany.

The Lt. seems to be an alright guy.

I still didn't answer all your letters but I will.

Don't worry about getting the camera?

I will sign off until I get straightened out here . . .

The first American troops entered Heidelberg on Friday, March 30, 1945, and the city surrendered without a fight. The Lieutenant mentioned was Donald H. Dearborn, who was awarded the Silver Star (Dearborn, Donald H. HQ, 34th Infantry Division, G.O. No. 99 [1945]).

Sunday 11 (Nov)

Well finally I received a letter that is one for this week + this one was 10 days old.

We had our first snow last night + it is still snowing a little bit

Every day is a day nearer Christmas they say we get 4 days off for Thanksgiving but we aren't doing anything anyway.

Got our ration yesterday for 2 weeks. 20 cigarettes 20 candies 5 gum + 2 cigarettes + I bought some hair tonic 1 wash rag 1 towel + it cost $4.05.

I think I'll try +sell my gun if I can now that they wont let us carry them anymore.

It cost me $40 so if I can get it back I will + send the money home.

Are you getting the bonds o.k.?

Those 3 Christmas packages I have worry me. Every day I look at them + wonder what is in them. In one I can here the bottle go "guggle"

You said they are shipping the guys over as soon as they are drafted well the only thing we have seen or heard of them is that some were suppose to come over.

They are getting these guys here to reenlist right + left. They have posters all over with a picture of the statue of liberty + would you like 90 days at home. Other ones with security retirement free Medical Care + all that stuff. I don't know maybe it would be or is smart for these guys to reenlist. But I want to get out + grab some of this cash that is going to be lying around.

Monday 12, (NOV)

Well I feel better now I received 2 letters from you + 1 from Dolly + Janet + the Mirror.

Now before we get any further In the morning I'm going to take a Lt. to Paris + stay for 7-9 weeks so I don't exactly know what I'm doing. It's some kind of Detached Service for 7-9 week driving Jeep, that's all.

Got daddy picture + the guys think he looks pretty rugged.

Glad to get a letter from Dolly tell her I'll write Some day?

I'll have to sign off now.

Still write to here + maybe I'll get a new address

Don't worry about a camera

It 9:30 and I got to pack yet + be off at 7:30 so good night

Hope you are all o.k.

Nov. 14

Well as you know I am not receiving mail up here so I will tell you what's going on.

I'm with this Lt. Dearborn at 7th Army Hd. Where there are so many Generals + colonels + all other officers that if you see a P.F.C. you think he's a P.W.

The lowest guy is a buck Sergeant

When this Lt. gets organized we are going to outfit going home + he is suppose to check there records + help them get ready to get set.

He says we will be traveling all over Germany.

I've got my own jeep + he lives in a hotel in Heidelberg + I'm out in the edge of town.

So as you can see I take the jeep + carry him around + at night it is mine. I take it + travel it around. Just got back from a show with Fred Mac. Its Murder He Says. I get all the gas I want + just have to sign for it.

This Lt. is also a wolf when I picked him up after dinner he had two WAC. Lts. with him.

He says Friday night we are going to go back to Hall for the weekend + some other week he wants to go to Belgium.

I guess I will get along o.k. with him.

Nov 15

Heidelberg

Well my Lt. went in the building + come out about 8 minutes later + said to take off he had been fired so I guess that's that.

We are suppose to go to Hall tomorrow if he don't get hired back.

Haven't seen the sun in the last 10 days expect it to snow good one of these nights.

Well I've been overseas 7 months now + 15 more days I'll be in 1 yr.

If they pass that 2 yr. stuff I'll be in a fine fix but I still think I'll be home in July.

I sure hope all of you are O.K., I'm O.K.

I kinds hate to go back to the company + start pulling guard again. This is the only kind of job to have in the army when the Lt. says pick me up at nine + pick me up for dinner + then about 4:30 + you can have the jeep tonight all this Detached Service is good. Now like tonight, he said drop by at 7, I might want to go to the officers club then you can go to the show.

I cant seem to find a helmet for Butch.

P.S. I forgot weather I asked you yesterday or not for some heavy socks.

Nov. 17

Hall

Well as you can see I'm back in hall + we made it o.k.

I cant understand the mail situation . . .

Coming from Heidelberg to Hall you have to go over a big hump, you start going up at Heilbronn + reach the bottom at Hall + they have about 4 -5 inches of snow on the top, but Hall is in a Valley surrounded by mountains + we have had only a little last Saturday.

How about another reading on the bank account + the bonds. Hope you got the last money order o.k.

I've been thinking about getting a transfer to service company +

start driving a 2 ½ again.

Slim, my buddie, has moved up + is driving the Major so he lives with him + Whittey is still in England.

We had our own click + now there isn't much doing.

If I only had some hopes of getting out of this Army.

I heard over the radio where all men now here will be out of here by Jan 1 1947 now that makes me feel very good.

Just 1 more long yr. seeing I was one of the last here+ believe it will be Jan 1 1947.

I had some hopes of making it by July but I guess not.

Maybe I should have signed up for 1 yr. last month + got 30 days at home.

When I think about it I get all down in the dumps.

Do you realize there are still guys with 80-100 points still over here.

I should think the people would get on Congress' neck.

They have come up with something new now a mobile Bn. (Battalion).

Couple half-tracks 3 or 4 armored cars + some peeps + they are going to go all over Germany + so if they have a riot any place they will be able to get any place fast

One day they will be in one town + the next day another town.

Just got my washing back 2 heavy undershirts 3 light under shirts 3 shorts 1 towel 6 pr. Socks 5 hankerchiefs washed + pressed. I give the kid 2 candy bars + a pack of gum + he was very happy.

I'm sorry that my Lt. lost his job because I had a racket there even so we aren't doing nothing here.

Nov. 20

Didn't write yesterday + Monday because we were out on roadblocks stopping all traffic, checking them + sending them back because they had another "Talley Ho" going on searching houses etc.

Up till today I had received only 4 letters in 16 days but today I got 2 letters for you + 1 from Joan + a Christmas Card from Gram + Jean.

I don't remember if I told you Saturday or not but some guys must have got over here from the states because 250 came into the 771 Tk. B. + they are here in Hall with us. They ask more questions than you would think was possible.

Well today they made out money books to us so they figure we wont be able to send home more money than we make but they always had that so its just another waste of time

When I was up in Heidelberg all the fellows had 3 shots for the flu so I suppose I'll get mine one of these days.

Well if old Carl has his questionnaire he should just about make it in the army a year after me.

One of the fellows here got a dependency discharge + he said it is pretty hard to leave.

Well if they pass that 18 mo. service stuff I ought to be getting home in a yr from now.

Bob's comment regarding intense questioning by the 771 Tank Destroyer Battalion was consistent with their mission at that time. At the end of the war, the mission of the 771 was to clean up pockets of resistance in areas between the Rhine and the Elbe.

11-21-45

Hall

I got another package last night with the cigarettes from Carl. Thank him a lot + sock soap + candy+ thank you a lot.

They just took the first Sgt. away in the Ambulance, hes got something.

I just thought maybe I'll be sending Carl cigarettes before long.

Remember when I thought I was coming home well I'm glad I didn't because I would be in japan now sure as the devil.

I'm pretty lonely now that Slim is driving the Colonel maybe Whittey will be back Sunday. It will make 3 weeks that he has been gone + it suppose to take from 3 -4 weeks.

Don't worry about the camera. I just got a notion one day but I guess it would be a nice thing to have. If you have to pay over $15 don't get one.

Hope you have received the money order O.K. How about a count on what I have?

You know if you would send me 3 -4 carton of cigarettes a month I could send home my full pay + have plenty to smoke because you can get $25 a carton + they cost $2. Twenty cents for postage + that leaves profit of about $22.70 or something like that. Say I get paid $40. Well I can only send home $44 but I could always get somebody else to send some home for me. Everybody else is making money so I might as well get some of it too.

Who won the checker game Doll or Carl?

I will sign off now with lots of love + Keep July on your mind.

Love

Bob or No. 1 son.

November 23

Ulm, Germany

I didn't write yesterday because it was thanksgiving + today we moved to Ulm so we wont get any mail today either.

We had a good dinner yesterday enclosed find the menu + plus that we had wine + champagne. I also was kept pretty busy packing + getting ready to move.

I guess we come south about 70-80 miles + although we just got here we are up like Ft. Tryon park + this looks like a pretty good size joint I mean city. We have pretty good billets. I have a room as big as our living room all to myself, have my cot+ is got a nice sofa, a rickety table + bureau.

Maybe we'll stay here a while.

I'll sign off now have to eat supper.

Nov 24

. . . got a package tonight with a carton of Old Golds, candy, writing paper thanks. It had October 12 paper in it.

Well tomorrow morning we are going to have another Talley Ho + I am going out on another road block for 24 hrs.

Monday I start driving jeep for Message Center + I won't have to pull any more guard. Only thing I have to pull Bn. Charge of Quarters once every 2 weeks or so.

It's getting pretty cold to drive but they are getting all the jeeps enclosed with Plywood so that it makes it pretty warm.

I'm eating your peanuts as I write.

Had a little snow last night.

My buddy Whittey is still in England, its about time he came back.

Slim had the Colonel's jeep last night + we rode around till 10:30.

This here message center jeep driver is you have to go around to all the companies every day there is 6 + go to Heidenheim to CCB. That's Combat Command B.

Operation Talley Ho was a Counter Intelligence Corps operation held in July 1945 to speed up the capture of Nazi war criminals still in hiding. This effort was led by the 7th Army, and Bob's unit was asked to assist. The project included a detailed sweep of the entire occupation zone in southwest Germany and was designed to discover contraband and root out war criminals and former German soldiers still at large.

Bob's photographs of the war—including the destruction of the city of Ulm—depicted many of the consequences of the war. There were bombed-out buildings, people living in the streets, and people pulling wagonloads of their furniture and possessions. He took photos of concentration camps, POWs, and displaced persons. His pictures were donated to, and can be viewed at, the George A. Smathers Libraries at the University of Florida in Gainesville.

AWOL is the official military term meaning that you are not where you are supposed to be at the time you are supposed to be there. Disappearing and desertion are the two most common ways to go AWOL, but it can also refer to other, simpler acts such as missing a medical appointment or being late for work. Whitey seemed to be AWOL on a constant basis; his behavior seemed to form a predictable pattern—he would perform his duties as a soldier for a period of time, then disappear for a while, only to be found in some other city or in a hospital. After a period of military incarceration, he would repeat the process.

November 30, Ulm, Germany

Dear Butch

I am sorry to hear that you have had trouble with your teeth and hope you feel O.K. now.

I been looking for a German helmet for you but they are pretty hard to find but I will get one before I come home

Hope you had a good Dinner on Thanksgiving we had a pretty good one.

I want to wish you a happy birthday but I cant figure out how old you are. I guess you'll be pretty big when I get home.

I guess you know I bought a German Pistol, it's a Mauser + shoots a Caliber 32 bullet. I believe I shall bring it home when I come.

I('m) driving a jeep regular now but it's pretty cold

I will sign off now with lots of love

Love

Bob

DECEMBER 1945—THE BLACK MARKET

Dec 1, 1945

Well a yr ago today was a pretty busy day. I wonder what it will be next yr? because I've been driving jeep all day today + got paid $35. I will send another money order when I get time. I've got $47 German + about $11 French+ I am able to send home about $60 but I will keep $20.

It's getting pretty cold freezing just about all the time.

My buddy Slim is taking the colonel's wife to Le Havre tomorrow so she can go home.

Whittey still didn't come back.

So I guess I'll be alone for a while.

I got a ¾ coat now with a fur liner + a hood, it's pretty warm. When I get the camera I shall take some pictures in it.

There is suppose to be the Largest no not Largest but the tallest church in the world here in Ulm+ the Danube river runs through here too. Most of this town is "Kaput" but what is left is pretty nice.

They have even got street cars running here. Got 2 nice clubs one for the N.C.O.s + its just like a high class joint in N.Y. + the E.M. Club isn't as good but it's alright. They also have a theatre + a Red Cross Club.

No mail tonight.

I will sign off after I ask for a package. You say to ask for one in every letter but you don't have to take it to heart.

Hope I get the camera pretty soon+ don't forget to take some money + get everybody something for Christmas.

Love

No. 1 son

You had better notify Butch he is No.2 (II) son

P.S. Send a package

12-2-45

They found somebody going to CC "B" so I haven't got anything to do. On days like this I think I'm going batty because I get to thinking to much about nothing.

Did I ever ask you for some more combs??

They have a play here in town tonight "three is a family". Maybe I'll go see it.

Slim left this morning for LeHavre with the Colonel + his wife said he will be back in 5 days. I guess they'll spend a day in Paris.

Did you hear about be able to get a discharge after 4 yr service? Why that is preposterous. (big word).

Well I hope I get the camera pretty soon.

I will sign off in a down hearted mood + go to the Red Cross.

December 3,

Ulm, Germany

Well its been a pretty nice day today everything went according to schedule

Turned my jeep in to get it enclosed.

They make a pretty nice job on them. They enclose them with plywood so I wont be riding so cold after all this winter.

Tried to make a money order today but they wasn't taking them. So I'll have to wait I guess.

I can see where I never want to live alone now that Slim is gone I *have only the radio to talk to.*

Tomorrow night I pull Bn. Change of Quarters. P.F.C. Glover looked pretty lonely on the list with all those Sgts + Cpls but I guess he can make out alright. All you have to do is sit in the Bn. C. P. + answer the phone + if anything important comes up, I call the Duty Officer where they call me the Duty Noncommission Off.

I think I'll go to the play "3 is a family" to night.

Seen the picture "You can't live forever" at the Red Cross last night. Pretty good.

No mail yesterday as it was Sun. + it hasn't come in tonight yet.

This afternoon I took the jeep as there was nothing to do + went all over hell looking for a helmet for Butch. Either they never had any here or they have hid them all for the next war.

I've watched about 40 men + a steam shovel + about 4 or 5 German trucks, ever since we have been here in Ulm, trying to clean up a sq. block that was a big pile of rubble+ it don't even start to look like they have worked yet. In about 10 yr. I think they will have everything cleaned up. I don't give a damn if they never get it cleaned up. Just add 6 points to 19 + you receive 25. I'm beginning to get up in this world.

One thing I would like to know is how old will Butch be tomorrow?? 8-9 or 10??

Enclosed is 10 French Franks. Keep it around some day we will look back to that year 1945 its worth $20 if you can trust the French?

Whittey is still AWOL. I guess he must have liked England.

He left just after getting that 3 month pay so I guess he is having a good time. He didn't care about anything much.

P.S. Please send a package.

Charge of Quarters is a military term for the responsibility of a US serviceman to stand guard, typically at the front entrance to the barracks.

It was often a twenty-four-hour period of responsibility for an NCO and an enlisted man, who monitor incoming and outgoing traffic. Other duties included radio checks and bed checks to ensure that servicemen were in bed and not AWOL.

Bob joked about being the only NCO in a group of senior soldiers, and indicated that he enjoyed the role—especially his unofficial new title of "Duty Noncommissioned Officer," a play on words.

Dec.

I'm still worried about what you were thinking when I asked you for that scarf. Let's forget about the whole thing.

I had to go to Division at Gumnal, it is over 50 miles one way so I am pretty tired.

I will tell you what about 7 pr was in the 2 packages. Socks 2 boxes of candy 1 carton cigarettes 5 bars of soap 2 combs + a Christmas tree.

I'm still trying to get a money order made out but the longer I wait the less it will be. Its down to $35 now you never did write + tell me . . . write + tell me how much money I had in the bank + how many bonds I have.

Just heard Fibber Magee + Molly it comes a week late.

Well here it is Wednesday morning 9 o'clock, I fell asleep last night with my pants on + Slim said he tried to wake me up but I didn't.

We haven't gone anyplace in the last couple of nights we generally go to the Club or the Red Cross.

We have a table top here nail on top of an orange crate + the table top has a checker board on it so we play checkers a lot.

I wonder if I'll be able to go to work again we are having it to easy here now. I think I wont want to do any more than sit in an office.

I'll bet that if I don't go to work as soon as I get home I never will want to go to work.

I will sign off now if you please with lots of love

Just bought $2 worth of stamps so that money order is getting smaller + smaller.

P.S. Send a package.

In addition to painting, knitting was another hobby that Louise enjoyed; she also was very productive in her spare time, knitting woolen hats, scarves, sweaters, blankets, etc. The scarf meant different things to Bob's family than it meant to him, and there was a misunderstanding about either the type of scarf or the colors that Bob wanted.

Dec. 5

First of all both of my arms are stiff an acheing I got 2 shots in 1 + in the other 1 for flue + 2 boosters for something.

Received 2 letters tonight one from you dated Nov 26 + one from Janet dated Nov 24. Also the pictures of the kids they are pretty good.

Enclosed are a couple of me + another kid that works in the Message Centre. If I get the camera you will get plenty of pictures.

Snowing pretty good. Went + got my enclosed jeep it's even got a dome light + I'm going to put electric wind shield wipers on.

Well that's enough for tonight as my arms are out of condition

Cant send money order yet.

Dec. 6, 1945

Received a letter from you Gram Mac + Janet + a Christmas Card from Doll + Miss Bush. In your letter I got the clasp but now I cant find the bracelet but I guess it is around some place.

Well I put an electric wind-shield wiper on my jeep today all I need now is a radio + a heater.

Been snowing just about all day.

. . . I'm to tired to concentrate.

Dec 12

Well I must apologize for not writing but I have been under the weather with a cold but I am O.K. again.

I have received 3 packages since I last wrote to you + several letters. The packages were candy one was a repacked one + I got the camera alright. Took a picture of Whittey under a light + that has been the only one since it has been snowing pretty near every day + the sun hasn't been out.

Maybe this is what made me sick.

I had my 2 Christmas packages in a corner + I come home the other day +they were gone. I hope the stuff in them was rotten.

Only me + Slim know about it so maybe somebody will make a slip+ say something.

We got about 8 more news guys in the company from the states.

Today is my day off so I'm just loafing around + it is snowing as usual.

Cant send any money yet they have got everything screwed up with this currency control books + other stuff.

> *You say that there is a lot of people out of work maybe it would be wise to stay in the army you get 3 meal(s), good pay free medical + dental care + a good retirement. That's what the posters say anyway.*
>
> *I thought this was going to be an exceptionally long letter but I cant think of anything. Thanks a lot for everything + hope all of you people are alright. I am feeling good as ever again.*
>
> *Wish I could send my money home.*
>
> *There isn't much black market in this town. Hall was the place for that.*
>
> *I will take some pictures if the sun ever comes out.*
>
> *Just got my washing back. Two little kids a boy + a girl they carry it for about a mile.*

The inability to send money home became a serious subject for Bob and millions of other US soldiers. It was also a very complicated issue for the US Military, which was attempting to control the flow of currency as well as putting an end to black market trading.

The Allied Forces' inability to control the flow of currency came to a head in 1945. As US Army soldiers moved into Germany, they accumulated German marks, with the belief that there was a certain value to them. Soldiers anticipated that they could trade their German marks into US dollars at a later date.

Therefore, as the value of the German mark continued to drop to new lows, entrepreneurial soldiers bought more and more of the devalued marks with dollars on the black market; then they would trade them for profitable items, which they later converted back into dollars.

Initially, to gain control over the trading, the US Army artificially fixed the exchange rate of dollars to marks at a higher rate than the marks were worth; in hindsight, this was a huge mistake. The Allies began to issue "Allied marks" which were perceived as more stable and had a higher value than the German marks.

American soldiers quickly discovered the significant imbalance in the "real" market rates versus the artificial rates, and they profited significantly by trading German marks and US dollars. The Army soon realized their mistake in fixing the exchange rate, and to stop what could be a flood of marks and dollars sent home to the United States, the military decided to limit the number of dollars a soldier could send home. The intent was to discourage soldiers from temporarily trading and accumulating excessively large amounts of marks. Simply put, the military now oversaw any currency a soldier sent home. This policy caused resentment among the soldiers who had been profiting significantly through trading. In addition to the perceived harsh policy, due to the artificial exchange rates, the US Army was now being criticized for "promoting" the conversion of the often-looted German marks into US dollars.

On April 19, 1945, the Army changed their policy regarding currency exchange and ordered military post offices and PXs to stop accepting the marks as payment for purchases. By V-E Day in June, the Army mistakenly believed the currency control problem was over, and it reversed its decision, allowing soldiers to once more send large amounts of money back to the United States. If there was any concern that a soldier might have illegally converted marks into dollars—evidenced by the large amount of dollars he was sending home—all the soldier had to do was explain that he had a large amount of gambling profits, and the Army accepted this explanation at face value.

However, the German mark continued to drop in value, and US soldiers continued to make illegal profits through trading. Russian soldiers also got into the practice of black market trading, which accelerated the problem.

By July 24, the US Army realized the problem had returned and was greater than they had feared. Clear proof that there was a problem was the fact that US troops had drawn one million dollars in pay the previous month, and yet had somehow sent four million dollars home.

The US Army had another currency problem to manage; they needed to obtain actual US dollars for soldiers to convert the newly issued Allied marks. The black market had grown huge, and there were millions of Allied marks in the market. Soldiers who held Allied marks, would eventually demand to exchange them for dollars when they were ready to return home.

The US Army believed the solution was to stop issuing Allied marks and to issue currency control books to create a record of the soldier's finances. On November 10, 1945, each enlisted man was issued a book to record his cash on hand and his bank deposits. All new monetary transactions were to be entered in the book; the idea was that when the soldier was ready to return home, he was entitled to exchange only the net amount of dollars listed in the book. Officers were responsible for certifying each entry and initialing each transaction. This also became a weak and cumbersome practice for the military to manage.

The currency control situation was eventually curbed, but the process was neither quick nor clean.

Dec 14

Well the sun is out today for about the first time in a week so I will try to get some pictures

I'm going to get a $35 money order made out.

I still haven't got over somebody stealing my packages.

Received a letter from Dolly yesterday

The three of us went + got a case of beer yesterday for 20 bottles of beer + the case it cost $0.70

I wish I had something to write this is like pulling teeth.

I'm on C.Q. again tonight so I will try again then.

December 14

Here we start on the second letter for today for as you can see by the paper I am on C.Q.

We will have to wait a couple of weeks to make out a money order —so says the mail man- hope I have some money left by then because Slim + Whittey are broke. Every time I turn around its money for cleaning or beer or something but as long as it is those guys it is alright.

Took 1 roll of film today+ four on another one so all we have to do now is to get them developed + I will send them home they are all with us 3.

I wish you could meet these guys. All of us are crazy + the first Sgt. knows it the way he talks.

All the army is, is to know the right people + you will get ahead. I guess the whole world is like that.

When they put up the names for Bn. C. Q. they have a column of Duty N.C. O. + Duty Officers so I am the only P.F.C. pulling Bn. C.Q. so the other day I called the captains attention to that + made a joke out of it + gave him a general hint.

Well we shall now wander off of that subject.

Did I tell you in one of the packages I got there was a bottle of Vaseline Hair Tonic. The first I got since I asked you for it.

I will sign off now + keep the packages sailing.

Dec. 16th, 1945

Dear Mom,

I received a letter dated Dec. 9 last night so we will try to answer it.

Don't worry about these Krauts, they aren't having any trouble with them now.

I turned in two rolls of films to get developed + will get them back in 4 days. Then I will send some pictures home.

I'm sorry to hear about Sarno.

Glad to hear Jeanie has a job + I cant see where $.75 is bad. I've worked for less.

I got the clasp for the Identification bracelet. I am wearing it now.

What kind of idea did you get when I asked you for a scarf? Well I just thought I would look sharp. Green is for armored like blue is for infantry. A Khaki colored one will be O.K. if you are worried?

Us three raise more hell with these Hinnies than a whole army.

Glad to hear about Carl. THIS ARMY WILL MAKE A MAN OUT OF HIM. HA HA

I will have to write Butch and congratulate him on the election. He must be quite a character. I don't remember of ever being vice-president or anything else.

He'll probably be the Mayor of N.Y.C. by the time I get home.

Where did my sister get the idea that I don't read half the letters you send?

I like my job alright. I'm in with the right people anyhow. I've even got the Lt's giving me drinks.

There are two big Lts' from Texas + with that southern talk + I give them that Bklyn accent + we have a pretty good time.

When I take the messages in to the Cornel's office, he even says good morning once in a while. Every time I see him he looks more like Dad.

That Navy Yard better not hire to many guys because one of these days I plan to cut some guy out of a job when I come home.

I never got over that plastic stuff + if we could arrange it with the navy yard so I could go to school at the Gov't expense (G.I. Bill of Rights) and take up these plastics. But maybe I should wait till I see what turns out in the Navy Yard. I believe when I get home I will be lazy as heck because I don't do any hard work here.im worried that I might not take the right step.

I guess a Gov't job is as good as you can get.

That's enough of that. I might not get out of here for another year.

I will sign off + don't get any ideas of scarfs, send package.

Do you read my letters?

The three of us are going to take the Jeep + our carbines + go deer hunting.

They have taken my pistol + I cant get it till I leave the 1st Armored or come home.

Dec 18

Dear Butch

Congratulations on being Vice president of your Class. I don't remember of ever being anything like that.

I think I've looked all over Germany for a Helmet but I cant find

> *any.*
>
> *How are you making out? Mom tells me you are pretty big now.*
> *There isn't much to write about*
> *I just wanted to write + congratulate you.*
> *Love*
> *Bob*

Because of the war effort, there was a shortage of several materials, like natural rubber. New technology developed novel materials, particularly plastics like polyvinyl chloride, low-density polyethylene, polystyrene, and polymethyl methacrylate, which were adapted for military use by both the Germans and the Allies. Polyethylene was used in radar components in the early 1940s, initial production of poly (vinyl chloride), PVC-based products, and Super Glue (methyl cyanoacrylate) was discovered in 1942 by Eastman Kodak. In 1943, Teflon (methyl cyanoacrylate) came into commercial use.

Bob became aware of this growing market during his time at the Navy Yard, and he wondered if the industry would be an opportunity for employment upon his return home.

In 1938, during the Great Depression, the federal government set minimum wage rates under the Fair Labor Standards Act, 1938 - 2009 for the year 1945 at $0.40 per hour. Cousin Jeanie was earning almost double that rate.

> *Dec 18, 1945 (addressed to Mr. Roy Glover)*
>
> *I received two packages tonight mailed the 26+29 of Nov. So they are making pretty good time. Thanks a lot. It puts an extra kick in me when I get a package.*
>
> *The German never brought my film back today like he was*

suppose to. Maybe he'll bring them tomorrow.

Everything is just about the same.

Slim made Corporal for driving the Cornel.

I hear over the radio you are having a lot of bad weather.

It is pretty cold here but it hasn't snowed in a couple of days. About a mile from hear they are blowing up a big underground factory so all day long you are shaken.

I was thinking Carl would maybe get in the 1st Armored but we have got filled up on those last guys that come over.

Tell him if he comes this way to write + tell me where he is. I have the whole German telephone system in Message Centre + I will call him up or if he isn't to far I will go see him.

Heinrich Himmler, Head of the German SS, was convinced that Germany should take advantage of that country's many caves for defensive and manufacturing purposes.

Plans were developed and forced labor was used to build several massive underground facilities; the total size of these facilities was larger than the state of Rhode Island.

Many war-related activities had taken place in the mines; the Richard Mine, for example was a huge underground facility with thirty kilometers of underground passages. It was converted into a reinforced underground production facility, which manufactured the German Tiger Tank.

Dec. 20

First of all I got the pictures back as you have already noticed. Some are pretty good + others aren't so hot.

The letters I wrote yesterday I think I dated the 18 so I get all messed up upon my days.

I like the pictures. Have taken another roll but will have to wait to get them developed.

Was a pretty warm day today but I expect to see a blizzard any day.

I believe if Arthur Sarno does get back to the states he'll never come back over here. Haven't gotten any mail in the last couple of days.

The colonel told Slim he thought guys would spend 3 years over here before they would get discharged

With that thought in your mind I remain ever your son.

Christmas

Received a letter from you . . .

Still didn't get around to making out a money order.

Why did you ever write poor kids on that clipping. They are the sucker(s) that have to come over here so some of us can get home.

This day being Christmas I feel very low it don't seem like Christmas just another day. I hope I am home for next Christmas although I have been considering (don't get excited) just thinking about taking a Gov't Civilian job over here. You can get up $50 a week + it wouldn't cost much to live but I will wait + see what is going on back in the states. The only trouble is they will not let you go home + then come back + take a job . . . but we shall wait + see what turns up.

Maybe I think to (o) much?

I will sign off now + write tomorrow as it is my day off.

> *Christmas*
>
> *Dear Dad,*
>
> *Well here I am again another Christmas away from home. I hope there wont be another one.*
>
> *We don't write to each other very often but I figure I write everything to mom + I guess you figure the same way around.*
>
> *As you probably know I am driving Message Centre jeeps now + I am kept pretty busy. Have Wednesday s off+ pull Bn. C. Q. once every 12 days or so.*
>
> *Every morning I work on my jeep from 8 to 8:30 then take the Stars + Stripes to the Red Cross at 9:30 + have coffee + donuts + at 11. I take stuff to the Companies (6) City Jail, UNRRA, Miltary Gov't., 910AAA 356 T.A. + other places then at 4, I go to CC"B" at Heidenheim which is 25 miles + then I'm finished.*
>
> *It isn't too bad got a pretty good Sgt. + there is no officer direct in Charge but . . . Lt. Swope is O.K + that keeps everything on the ball.*
>
> *We had a pretty good dinner today but it don't seem like Christmas every day is just about the same over here. Its just a wait till they get ready to send you home.*
>
> *I will sign off now*
>
> *Love*
>
> *Bob*

Bob was impressed with his Lieutenant's ability to lead the unit. Lt. Richard Swope was attached to the 4th Armored Regiment that headed into Bastogne to relieve the 101st Airborne division, and eventually was encircled during the Battle of the Bulge. Lt. Swope earned a battlefield commission and was awarded the Combat Infantry Badge, Silver Star, Bronze Star, two Purple

Hearts, ETO ribbon, four Battle Stars, Good Conduct, and the WWII Victory medal.

As part of his job, Bob now traveled to the United Nations Relief and Rehabilitation Administration (UNRRA) facility to deliver mail. UNRRA was established in November 1943; its mission was to repatriate and support refugees at the war's end. The civilian relief teams of UNRRA were charged with coordinating relief efforts and managing the refugee camps.

UNRRA was also responsible for certifying welfare agencies in the camps. In late 1945, UNRRA oversaw management of the displaced persons (DPs) and relations with the central and camp committees. The expansive effort cost the United Nations billions of dollars and eventually resulted in the insolvency of the UNRRA.

December 30

Ulm, Germany

No mail today as it is Sunday so we shall struggle along on the facts we have.

I am trying to think what to write.

Everything went along pretty good today not much trouble with the jeep.

It is snowing again but melting pretty soon as it hits.

I am eating your girl scout cookies with peanut butter on them "pretty good"

They claim that the 50 pointers are going to start home next month.

I've got all the family's pictures stapled on the wall over my bed.

How did you ever send such a big box?

Everytime I look around another day has dragged by + I wish they would drag a few by when I wasn't looking.

Gas is hard to get over here every vehicle is rationed.

Well I guess I will close off now with lots of love + more pictures.

Dec. 31

Received six letters tonight two from you + Janet 1 from Jean + Butch.

It don't matter what kind of Scarf you send me.+ you can hook a pr. of gloves if you want to but don't pay to much for them.

What is this Jungle rot?

I got the jeep so it runs halfway right now.

Seeing as tonight is New Year's eve I am again wondering where I will be next year at this time. I think I'm getting so it don't make much difference.

The 45 pts. Guys are going to leave next month so they are working around to my level. So maybe I wont rot over here yet.

Whitey is trying to get drunk on German beer. What a life.

1946

JANUARY 1946—ULM, DRIVING THE JEEP

Jan 2

Well I am in a little better mood today after working on my jeep most of the day+ it goes a little better.

No mail today a couple of ton burned up some maybe there was some in there for me

Got paid today $35. I've got $60 now that I will be able to send home about $45+ got a deal with Whitey to send home $30 to you for me. I don't know how it will all turn out. I think I'm turning into a miser or a schrew article?

When you send a letter drop a nickel in 2 or 3 of them + I got some connections to make rings + bracelets. I'll make something out of this vacation yet.

If you can get the material you can get things made.

You have been sending me 620 film instead of 120.

Tell Butch I have got a German helmet. Got it painted green + it looks O.K. Slim made the connection. I'll get a box made + send it home soon as possible. It took a long time but finally got it. They have got all this German equipment lock up.

If everything works out alright we might get rich yet. HA HA

The money situation will drive me crazy yet.

Jan. 6, 1946

Nobody is getting any mail so I guess everybody is taking a vacation.

Got the box yesterday but it is big enough for 2 helmets so I will try + steal another one today. I am not finished Charge of Quarters till 12 o'clock. It is real cold out today but the sun is out so maybe it will get warmer

This place is always short on matches so maybe you could hook me a lighter some place a cheap one because I'll probably lose it in a week + you can send some summer underwear if you can get some.

I guess I told you that Slim is going to take the colonel to LeHavre tomorrow + when he comes back we are going to try + get a pass someplace together

I imagine he + I would have quite a time.

The Sgt. Major worked for the company that built bldg no. 3 in the navy yard. He's quite a character his name is Conroy + just as Irish as they come.

How is Jeanie making out. I've been worrying if she ever found a job.

I was looking at life magazine + they had a big 2 page picture of the fleet + I could practically see our house.

How is our co-friend Carl making out. I guess he will be coming over pretty soon. But this army needs good men? HA HA

You might as well forget about the scarf because before it gets here it will be summer.

Them nickels I told you to send wont be any good it will have to be quarters.

If they pass that bill of 2 years of service do you realize it will be next Christmas or after before I get out. Now if they had it 18 mos. I would practically have this army whipped. But I guess I'm lucky I am still alive.

I wish the major would keep his nose out of here. He keeps on hinting that I should build a fire. He just come over from the states so he don't worry me a bit.

Whittey told him of New Years when he was on guard. The fire is now roaring + I am all dirty.

This is a funny job I have to be an auto mechanic + a office worker at the same time sometimes I have to take a message into the Cornel + I go in all dirty+ greasy + he looks at me with one eye + goes on working. See you someday.

Jan 8, 1946

Received 2 letters + another package last night thanks a lot. I've got over $100 now + you will either receive a brand-new camera or $30. From Whittey I can only send home $90 but I can always get a hold of some stamps+ send home. Let me know if you can cash them home.

Haven't sent the two helmets yet. I don't have much time during the day for stuff like that + to make out a money order but the money is just accumulating.

In the package there was a carton of cigarettes + candy.

If you don't have money to buy stuff for the packages take it out of the bank

What pictures did you frame?

Despite the US military's efforts to control currency, Bob found creative ways to send money home. It helped to have good friends like Whitey to assist in this noble effort.

Jan 8, 1946

Letter No 2

Just received a Christmas Card + a letter from you dated Dec.19

Did you hear about this stuff where Paterson said he couldn't get replacements? Well that must be a lot of Bull-Everybody over here has just about blew a fuse today over that.

I guess the whole army over here is discussed (disgusted) now. All the 50 pt. men were expecting to leave the 15 of this month now they will have to stay up to 3 months more. I think I'll be lucky if I ever get home.

The spirits you sent were stolen.

"Now that my Darling is going away" maybe some other darling can get home. Christ you cant feel that bad about it there are still some guys here who have been in the Army pretty near 4 years + the God damn war's over.

I think that is how the whole public feels + don't give a damn who is left over here.

Glad to hear that the navy yard is looking out for its men anyhow.

Bob's frustration is now evident in his letters. He is sympathetic to the soldiers who have earned enough points to return to the States, but at the same time, he wishes that he could qualify too.

It is no surprise that the "Patterson Request" drew so much attention from the American public and the servicemen overseas.

After F. D. Roosevelt died, President Harry S. Truman immediately began to publicly address the costs of the war—including waste and mismanagement—and he formed a committee to investigate and report. Roosevelt had been more patient on this than Truman; Roosevelt was concerned that morale would be hurt if it were perceived that the government was "closing the tap prematurely.

Robert P. Patterson, Undersecretary of War, asked Truman to delay any significant budget cuts and to delay investigations into misuse of spending. Patterson suggested that it was "in the public interest" to suspend the committee working on the project.

Truman gave his full support of the committee's work and publicly stated that their intent was not to criticize the use of resources by the military. Unfortunately, the damage had already been done, and many soldiers and their families became resentful of Truman, as shown in Bob's letter above.

Jan 9, 1946

Well it's Wednesday again, boy they seem to come pretty quick. I still haven't mailed the box yet or made out the money order.

The mailman says I'll have to wait to the 15(th) to make out the money order.

Everybody has cooled off a little bit about that 3 mo delay. They are now taking a "poll" over here of how much money a month a soldier would want to stay over here + enlist for 3 yr. If they give me a $100 a week I might stay here.

Me + Whittey stayed up in the room here last night + I thought we were going batty we would look at each other + listen to the radio.

There was a good chance for 2 guys to go to school for Mechanical Drawing but Whittey wouldn't go + I aint going someplace for 8 weeks by myself + I just wouldn't like it.

When Slim comes back he + I are going to try + get a pass to some place. I could get a pass to Switzerland but it cost $80 + that is 2 months pay.

The comments regarding his three-month delay were a result of other soldiers ending their service. Despite efforts by the government to convince enlisted men and women to remain on duty after the war ended, many just wanted to go home. The Army offered incentives like entertainment and education programs, which were well received; however, surveys conducted by the Army indicated that the "high point" men wanted to return to the United States and were becoming dissatisfied with the delays in the process. The men naively guessed that the main reason for the delay was a shortage of space on ships crossing the Atlantic. Eisenhower realized that the delays could potentially cause serious morale issues and ordered that, "Both officers and enlisted men will be fully informed of the reasons for delay in connection with their return home and no frivolous answers will lie given to any inquiry on this subject."

Jan 11, 46

No mail yesterday or today.

I heard over the radio where they are going to discharge men faster now that all these demonstrations are going on.

Nothing new.

Got 4 pictures but the other 4 didn't come out on account it was so dark the day we took them.

My jeep is running pretty good now.

Slim still didn't come back + Whittey's on Guard so I'm going to take a bath.

I hate to write on the back of a page because then it don't look like much.

You can send some cigarettes if you can scrape up the cash. I'll send the money soon as possible ($90) + Whittey said he would

---

make out a money order of $30 for you.

We have had pretty good weather so far.

The big question every guy has over here is when he'll get home? When.

January 13, 1946

No mail in quite a while but nobody is getting any so its O.K.

Snowing a little bit today I think we will have a blizzard one of these days.

I see where they say the soldiers over here need more work well maybe they do but the officers don't even want to work so what can they do + I see where they are going to get the men home as fast as replacements come. But that don't help me any if they would give a fellow a definite date or length of time he had to stay over here it would be better.

Don't worry, I'll still make it.

You can send some cigarettes if you want to. There isn't anything else besides that.

It seems to be getting harder + harder to write a letter because the same old stuff happens.

Well I got my 9 months in over here.

I just hope I don't get to lazy in this army you learn in this army to try + get out of doing things.

January 14

Received 6 letters tonight for a change. Sorry to hear that the mail is taking so long to get there but it is taking just as long to get there.

I never seen that Utility bag you were talking about + they also got the spirits.

You say not to re-enlist but I kind of think I should.

Glad to hear that you are getting the bonds O.K.

Got two letters from Janet + 1 from Butch + the pictures of them at the Halloween party.

This army isn't so bad now that I am in the right place.

I've got $135 now + Whitey is going to send 30 dollars to you when we can make out money orders. I can only send $90 out of the 135 so you let me know about stamps if you can cash them + send some cigarettes

---

January 16

No mail again today so this will probably be short + sweet.

It snowed for 3 days + now it is cold + when I say cold I mean it.

I bought a $15 watch today expecting to make a little money but sold it to Whitey at same price as he didn't have one. He left today for Hungary to go by train "cattle car" to guard P.W. who are going home. He is quite a character + I think a little "cracked".

Hope all of you people are o.k.

They are trying to suck more guys in quick by giving them till Feb. first if they want to hold their present rank.

The way things look I wont get out till next January.

I would like to be home right now but I don't know if I would be able to live a normal life again.

Now I am leading a pretty normal life I leave at 8 with Slim + he is waiting when I get home about 7

We went to the club last night we never seem to have any trouble when we go there maybe it is because he is just about as tall + a little bit heavier than I am + most of them seen him take care of one guy one night when one guy stole Whitey's hat. Whitey only comes up to my shoulder + is real thin so when he gets in trouble he comes to us.

Well that's enough for tonight so I will sign off.

Jan 22

It's been so long since I got any mail it isn't funny anymore.

I put in for a $50 money order today but I have another wristwatch + another camera I've only got about $30 left. I will either send the watch + camera home or sell them for money orders.

Everything is alright here hope it is the same home.

More fellows are shipping out to come home + they have got down to 45 pts.

Confidential I don't think there is a chance for me to get home till about next Jan with 2 years of service.

Well I guess that is about all till next time.

I am enclosing a picture of me + my jeep + note the sign in German says Charlie Chaplin in the Gold Rush.

SEND me a couple of quarters $.25

Jan 23

Received 4 letters today all from around Jan 9. Glad to hear you got the pictures

They shipped that 82 A. B. Div home a head of the 2 armored just for that parade.

Glad to hear they are still drafting fellows

Hope Carl likes it in the Army.

Whitey don't look like Van Johnson but Red Skelton

He got out of his AWOL with just a little extra duty. He is quite a character.

Slim is still around.

These Heinies are going batty by the minute they only want to give $20 a carton for cigarettes + you can get them to give $25. I am getting a new wallet off of one for a couple of marks next week.

I'm still driving the jeep + taking it easy because I'm afraid it will fall apart.

I'm getting a $50 money order made out + have a watch + a camera.

I never did mail the package but now I am going to send the watch in it + insure it for $50.

Well I'll sign off now a little discussed.

Jan 24

Nothing much new. Received a letter from Carl telling me his troubles. I'm waiting for him.

Still didn't get the money order back.

I expect to make t/5 before the month is up. It's in the bag but hasn't come thru yet. I put the screws to a Lt.

My jeep is giving me trouble once in a while

There isn't much to write about.

So I'll sign off this Letter was just to let you know I'm still alive.

Jan. 25

You have already found the money order so that is settled.

I received a big package with everything from soup to nuts it had a Dec 18 paper in it. It was the biggest one I ever got.

Thank you all.

You can take this money order + buy yourself something + send some more packages . . .

I sure do appreciate all of this stuff you send + all the trouble you go thru. So take this money + get something for yourself.

I was promised by the Sgt. Major to make T/5 by the end of the month. If it don't come thru I'll put the screws to somebody.

Whitey still didn't get back. Slim is still around.

This watch I'm going to send home loses a little time so you can get it fixed+ give it to dad it's brand new from Switzerland.

A Master Sgt named Conroy from Bklyn promised to call up Dolly when he gets home but all of these guys forget when they get home. He was a good egg.

Did I ever tell you about this room Slim + I have well over each bed we have our family pictures + the rest of the world + half the ceiling is covered with pin ups.

We both have double beds

We have a radio electric heater, alarm clock

I will sign off now with Beau coupe

Love

Bob

Bob's occasional request to be sent watches suggests he was interested in using them as resources to trade on the black market.

Jan 26

Ulm

Just received a letter dated Jan 7 glad to get all mail

I had never lost the thought of staying over here in a civilian job because of the pay but now they claim they are full. I guess when it comes right down to it I would refuse.

You could drive the jeep it(s) just like a car only thing you would have a little trouble getting in+ out. The job calls for T/5 + if I don't make it by the end of the mo.   I'm quitting. I was offered a job in Bn. S-2 but I doubt if I could stand an office job.

Everybody calls me Mr. Courier

Sent a $50 money order yesterday hope you get it O.K.

I am eating those mixed nuts you sent very good

As early as May 1945, President Truman stated that he wanted control of Germany to shift to a civilian responsibility as quickly as possible, and he believed that the US military should not have any governmental responsibilities. Truman and General Eisenhower met in July to firm up plans and agreed on the objective.

In September, a plan was announced to persuade US officers and enlisted men to remain in Germany as civilians. All military government activity was to stop as of December 31st. The details of the plan created quite a stir in Washington and in the field. On October 31, President Truman released Eisenhower's

186

letter to the press to put an end to the controversy and announced that the shift from military to State Department civilian control in Germany would be made by June 1946.

This goal was easier said than done. As the search began for US soldiers to volunteer for civilians jobs, many responded as Bob did in his letter, asserting that they did not want low level jobs and that they should let the Germans do it! A plan was then developed to include Germans experienced in politics and administration in the efforts to rebuild the country.

∞∞ ∞∞ ∞∞

In less than two years, Bob had risen through the lower echelon of ranks of enlisted men. When he first enlisted, his rank was Private; then he was promoted to Private, First Class. He was hopeful to be promoted again to Sergeant.

Enlisted men were supervised by non–commissioned officers (NCOs)—corporals and sergeants who were responsible for giving orders and ensuring they were carried out properly.

Sergeants wore chevrons on their stripes indicating their level of rank. Infantry units, starting in 1942, were enabled to promote assistant squad leaders to become sergeants, squad leaders to become staff sergeants, and platoon sergeants to become Technical sergeants. The higher pay that came with the increased rank was considered to compensate for the dangers of an infantry unit.

In 1942, the army recognized an increased need for soldiers with technical skills, and a new category of NCO was established. The letter "T" was added to the sergeant stripes to indicate that the wearer had special skills.

Sun. Jan 27

Well here we go again everything is just about the same. Been pretty cold here today + foggy.

No mail seeing that today is Sunday there was no mail.

I have never sent those helmets yet but I think I will get them off tomorrow if I have the time

I will put the watch in there some place so look through all the paper + inside the helmets when you get it.

When I write + tell you I've made T/5 for sure don't get all excited because I may not have it very long. It took a little pressure around but its in the bag.

There wont be but 20 of us in Message Centre that know its operations so I told the Sgt maj I was quitting if I didn't get it by the first. Don't think I aint working for it.

I have to report to the motor park at 8 A.M. + I am driving on + off till 7 P.M. Not steady but put on over 100 miles

It's a racket but you can make it look hard.

Well I shall sign off + you can send something if you feel like it.

Jan 29

Well I guess I haven't written in a week.

I received a big box tonight with 3 cartons of cigarettes jar of peanut butter, cookies, peanuts +combs + a wash cloth. Thank you very much there isn't much of a price for cigarettes here in Ulm. I have got $30 left from last month + it is pretty near payday so that isn't so bad.

There seems to be less+ less to write about. I have sat down several times trying to write but there isn't nothing to write about.

I've been having trouble with my jeep + I've received several "ass chewings" because of it + pretty near got into a fight with a sergeant. I can take just so much of that stuff+ then I blow my top. All I can think about is when somebody starts chewing is that guy has only a couple of stripes or a bar + in civilian life I wouldn't take it off of them.

I'll be glad when I get out of the goddamn army + when I do get out all I want is that paper + forget about it I wouldn't reenlist for the whole world.

I still haven't got cooled off yet. I don't think sometimes I get so mad I could tear everything apart.

I think there has been a big change in me since I've left home with my 19 pts. Home seems a long way off.

Whitey wrote Dolly a letter but sent it Tue I think.

Hope all of you are O.K. I am feeling alright again.

It's Sat night + I'd give anything I've got to get home.

Do you think it is possible to get home sick after being away from home so long.

I try to kid myself that I will be home for my birthday but if they keep the points or any other way I'll be lucky if I get out by next Christmas

I'll bet if Slim + Whitey wasn't around I'd go batty.

Enclosed are some more pictures + I will sign off now

Thanks again for the package.

Jan 29

I read in Stars + Stripes tonight where our mail is still in France from 2 weeks ago so I guess you are having the same trouble as me.

The package will be on its way as soon as I find some nails when you open it be careful because there is a watch in it inside of one of the Helmets. You probably wont get it for a month or more.

Write + let me know as soon as you get it + then I will send the camera or I may sell it to Whitey if he will make out 1 $30 money order to you. He still didn't get back from Hungary.

Jan 31

Well I made it mom I made T/5. I don't know how long I'll keep it but I will try + keep it long as possible + look for an opening to go higher. In case you don't know what it looks like: two stripes with a T under them.

Hope all of you are O.K. I am O.K.

Snowing again today. It snows pretty near every day but it don't amount to anything.

I'm on C.Q. again tomorrow night.

If I ever get some nails I'll send that box home. I will sign off now, no mail again.

Love
Bob

Bob's celebration was a bit premature. He may have been told that he was getting a promotion to T/5, but in reality, at this time, he was promoted to T/4. This promotion was an indication of his constant progress, but Bob may have been disappointed and expected more.

FEBRUARY 1946—PAYDAY

Feb 1, 1946

I'm on CQ. again tonight so I didn't go to Hiedenheim. There is a rumor going around that we might move. I hope we don't because I've got a good deal here. I haven't fallen out for reveille (Spell) since we've been here.

Some of the guys with as many points as I've got think we'll be home in the fall but I don't think they will ever cut it down to 18 mo. Service, I think that 2 yrs is low as they'll get. That would make me get home in just about a yr. I've been in 14 mo today + overseas 9 ½ months. All we can do is pray.

Let me know how Carl is making out.

Sent the money order Jan 25. Let me know when you get it.

Slim took the Bn. C. O. to Bad Tolz near Austria so he will be gone a couple of days he is kind of mad he says he gets home for a week + takes off.

Today was a clear day + you could see the Alp mountains from here.

Got paid today $39. Isn't much for a months work I'm going to hold on to it because I have been buying cigarettes for $20 a cartoon (spell) + selling them for $25.

There is all kinds of rackets here. You have just got to make the right connections.

The way I've been feeling lately I don't think I'll ever be able to work again. I'm getting Lazyer than ever.

I seen the letter dolly wrote to Whitey in the mail room.

That watch I bought from that sailor for $15 is still going + keeping perfect time I guess it was a real good one.

The crystal is a cracked up but otherwise it still is perfect.

Remember that wallet you bought me with my name on it well it looks like this now (drawing of wallet opening) ^UER suppose to be Bob Glover but its still holds together. I am getting one made by the Hienies.

I hate to do business with them because they look like they are thinking (that Son of a Bitch I'll get even with him). They hold out one hand for a cigarette + are wishing they had a knife in the other. They'll be another war they are getting back on their feet.

Any factory that is halfway usable they have going. I doubt if they will ever clean up some of these cities like here it is all just flat+ in 20 minutes of bombing —last yr. they killed 10,000 people here.

Feb. 3

Dear Dad

Just a line to let you know I'm still around.

I finally made something in the army it isn't much but it jumps the pay $14 a month.

They are planning on making this battalion a Cav. Outfit so then there will be a lot less ratings so I guess I will have a job holding what I've got.

The way it looks now there isn't any hopes of getting home for quite a while.

Them guys that left from the 106 + started for the Pacific are mostly discharged now they hit the states right when the war was over.

Well I will sign off now.

Love
Bob

Feb. 3, 1946

Received a big package last night that you mailed Jan. 5 so that isn't so bad.

It had 3 boxes of candy 1 carton cig, soap, peanut butter everything. Thanks a lot.

There is a great rumor going around that the 1st armored is going to bust up + they are going to make cavalry out of us. If they do I'll have to fight like hell to keep my T/5 but I think it is possible. There are a heck of a lot ratings in the cav. than in armored

You hear all kinds of stuff about going home but it gets you all excited for nothing. Heard a rumor that 9 out of 10 men here on V.J. day would be home by July.

Well thanks a lot for the package.

Feb. 4

Well the mail is starting to come in again it's caught up to Jan 20. I got 5 letters + another package tonight thanks a lot for everything. Boy you feel pretty good when you get a package.

First we shall get this underwear settled send white T shirts I guess 34 + white underpants same size no elastic in them

Break the news easy to Butch but I still haven't sent the box.

Tell him I cant get any nails + when I do send it will probably take a month.

Thank Dolly for the Valentines card I can tell her writing.

I've kind of forgot about re-enlisting. I guess you are right we should be together we damn shure don't like it like this + I guess if I signed up once I would keep on but I am kind of afraid of civilian life afraid that I might be a flop.

I don't know where Janet said that Dolly said that Whittey was handsome or not anyway over here you pick the guys you like + can trust. + I don't believe you can find two much better guys. Me and Slim have been living together practically ever since I've been in the first Armored + we have never had any trouble.

Sorry to here you aren't getting any butter we are getting enough I guess.

You said dimes in new envelope. No can find.

I can get some very nice Gold rings with diamonds in them for $75-80 bucks.

I'm still thinking it over

I bought that Swiss watch it only cost 2 cartons of cigarettes but I doubt if it will get home O.K.

Feb 8 1946

Haven't written any in a couple of days no excuse + I haven't received any in a couple of days.

Nothing new I would have lost my T/5 already if I didn't know the right people. A god damn Lt. from So. Co. turned me in for speeding but the Sgt. Maj. Got the adjutant to fix it up so its alright.

It said in tonights S+S that the 1st A. D. will be made Constabulary forces so maybe I'll have to change my address again.

Hope all of you people are well.

Had another typhus shot today. Some of the guys have got it so I guess they'll be watching carefully.

I was thinking today that I'll be an old man pretty soon. I'll be 20 before I know it + I still don't see any light of getting home before another yr. Maybe when I do get out I'll wish I was back in.

Well any way this is a good way to waste your life.

I've got it easy enough

I get up at 8-8:30 go to the motor park + fool around with my jeep + before you know it there goes another day.

Remember the night I left well then I thought I wouldn't be alive now so maybe I'm lucky as it is.

February 10, 1946

Ulm, Germany

Well I'm on C.Q. today so I hope this will be a long letter. No mail yesterday. I hope all of you are alright.

It tried to snow yesterday but melted as soon as it hit + today it is a nice sun shiney day.

I thought we would have a rough winter but we haven't had any snow or cold snaps to amount to anything yet+ I hope we don't.

Very good news in the papers last night that one hundred thousand new troops in E.T. by April.

They keep on doing that + I will get home one of these days. How is Carl making out?

Did Arthur ever get home?

I guess everything will be changed when I get there.

Time seems to be going pretty fast now that I have got a regular job. I've already got dissatisfied with that T/5 + I am looking for something better.

I don't know if I could get an easy job like I have got now or not. I have to pull this C.Q. every once in a while but otherwise it is only about 4 hrs driving + working on the jeep.

Slim just got my rations + the cost $20 but I won a watch + perfume. The watch is a 15 jewel Swiss watch with a sweep hand that knocks off 1/5 of Seconds. The name is Felca it only cost $9.90 but it is bought by the Govt. + then sold in these P.X. I also got perfume that cost $3.50 so you can see that I am going to need some money to balance my currency control book.

So send some when the only cost $2.00 a carton + sell for $25 or $30 you can lose anything.

Even if the money isn't up to par I've got 2 new watches + a new camera so —I would appreciate it very much if I got some cigarettes.

Seen the play Arsenic+ Old Lace last week. I don't remember telling you pretty good

I don't care much for plays.

Bob is learning how to make profitable trades, likely in the black market.

2/12/46

Just a short letter tonight + I will write tomorrow.

Just finished a letter to Carl.

Received a package mailed Jan 17 not bad 2 Valentines + a short letter from you.

You said you wasn't getting mail well nobody was for a while either way.

Received the scarf "tanks" + 2 pr of gloves + candy + cigarettes

Don't send no soap for a while have enough for a couple of months

Got plenty of towels + face cloths have plenty of all that stuff

You can send some "T" shirts + under wear + some more cigarettes

Also received the money

Feb 13

Well I was off all day + I be damned if I will again. I get to thinking of home + everything + get mad at everything.

I hope all of you are alright. No mail today.

Whitey is back as you know + he sat with me all day "bitching".

He is talking awful strong on re- enlisting.

Feb 14

Well here I go again trying to write you a letter.

Nothing new happen. I've got another guy helping me drive.

No mail today.

I didn't realize it till today but I'll have 15 mo in the end of this month + if they cut it to 18 months I'll have them.

Was pretty nice here today. The sun was out most all day.

Hope all of you are alright.

How did Carl ever get in the Air Corp?

Someday maybe I'll get Butch's Helmets off.

Sunday 15

No mail as it is Sunday so I don't know what kind of a letter this will be.

It has been raining today most all day + still is.

I've got an assistant driver now so I don't have to drive half the *time. He just came over is 27 has 2 kids name's Padberg + don't think much of me telling him what to do.*

If the breaks go right with guys transferring out I might have a possible chance to make T/4 that is if the right guys get put in the right places.

Slim took the Bn. C.O. some place today + still isn't back.

Well today is 10 mo overseas

I will be able to on 2 Hershey Bars pretty soon

Slim just come in so I will shoot the Bull to him.

Bob may have forgotten that in an earlier letter, he told his family that he was promoted to a T/5 rank. Apparently the orders had not been completed yet.

Feb. 16

Dear Doll,

Well after quite a spell I finally received a letter from you.

I feel sorry for you about your honey. But if there wasn't that honey+ plenty more I would never have a chance of getting home.

Lets keep that in your head.

Very few of these guys are here because they want to.

It will probably be a good thing for him + I don't believe it will be over 18 mo + the God damn air corp don't do anything anyhow.

I wrote him a letter after receiving one from him.

Couldn't read the address I hope it gets there O.K.

I feel sorry for him in a way but I cant help either of you.

Well lets drift away from that anyhow the war is over

Cant get any film over here so I guess you will have to keep sending it its 120 not 620.

Don't worry I don't think I'll re-enlist but sometimes I think I should.

It isn't so bad now.

Well I'll sign off.

Love Bob

Bob is making a point to his sister that if it weren't for newly enlisted men like her boyfriend, Carl, there would be no replacements to take over Bob's responsibilities and enable him to leave the military. So Bob is suggesting she shouldn't be too upset at the prospect of not seeing her boyfriend, since it would allow brother and sister to be reunited. Again, Bob is not thrilled with her relationship with Carl.

The phrase "Let's keep that in your head" is Bob's way of suggesting that this conversation is to remain confidential and only between them.

Bob's "don't worry . . . reenlist" comment is a bit of a braggadocio moment. Bob wants his sister to worry more about him and less about Carl.

Feb 18

Received 4 letters today, 2 from you, 1 Janet + one Gram Glover.

Been working on the jeep all day did everything to it that was possible so I am pretty tired tonight.

I don't remember what camera the pictures were taken with.

I have only taken one or two rolls.

That Greenport fire must have been quite a one.

Sorry to hear Janet was sick. Hope she is better now.

Carl must be having a hard time.

Received 3 quarters today bought a ring yesterday 16 mk. + silver + sold it for $6.00.

Remember I told you about getting another break well they have broke another way

Feb 20. 1946

Just received an old letter from you from Jan. 29.

Just got back from Heidenheim + on the way down the jeep broke down + I had to call in for another.

Had a little blizzard today for about half an hour.

Well when we go into this Cavalry I been promised Code Clerk + that will increase my rank one stripe.

I will sign off today + I am on C.Q. tomorrow you will probably get a long one.

Feb 19

Well everything went along alright today. Finished working on my jeep. It still rides like it is going to fall apart something is loose + I cant find it.

A couple of connections in the company are trying to get me Code Clerk, its still in message Centre but it calls for T/4. I can operate the machine.

Hope I can make it the T four is a Sergeant with a T under it. If I can make it maybe I'll be satisfied. "The more you get the more you want".

I was looking at myself in the mirror today + it looks like I am *getting to be quite a man. I guess I should be tough. I'll be 20 in July in case you have lost count.*

No mail today but there wasn't much for anybody.

Feb. 23

Received three letters tonight 2 from Janet + one from you. Yours was written on the third of February.

It is a quarter to twelve + I just finished getting back from CC "B" its been snowing for 3 days + the snow has drifted all over the roads+ they haven't used any snow plows yet.

Got stuck so many, it wasn't funny + I would have to wait till somebody came along.

Don't worry about re-enlisting.

I wont till I come home first.

Had a little blow out with the officer over Message Centre today so I doubt if I'll get that T/4. I had just finished cleaning up the jeep + I take some paper in the Battalions C.P. + he says that's a fine way to come in here + I blew my top

I will sign off + go to bed.

Bob's frustration continues to grow. He is becoming envious of other soldiers who are returning home. To add to his frustration, he now has a job with much greater responsibility, but without the promotion and pay increase that should go with it.

Feb. 28, 1946.

Today I am writing in the afternoon so I do not know if I will get any mail or not. Have not received any in the last couple of days.

Today is just like spring out most all that snow we had is gone.

I hate to tell you this but they say I cannot send home any more German equipment so I guess I cannot send helmets. Tell Butch I am sorry and they was not so good anyhow. Tell him I will bring home my pistol and he will be able to show that to his friends. It is a Mauser caliber .32.

Today is payday so as soon as possible I will send home a money order

There is not anything to write about so I will sign off for now

MARCH 1946—WHITEY GETS IN TROUBLE

March 2 1946

I have not wrote in a couple of days because I did not receive mail and just discussed with the whole thing.

I have been hijacked to go to France to bring back trucks and I would give anything to get out of it.

I got over fifty dollars so when I can I will make out a money order as soon as possible.

Had a chance to come home today for forty five days and come back for the minimum of six months. I figure when they offer you something like that it is not for your good. I did not know which way to do there for a while then slim said I had better not. Guess I did the right thing.

I know this is short but I will sign off

March 3

Dear Mom.

Going to Paris in the morning busy packing now

Love

Bob

Friday March 8

Just got back from France + washed up + found (4) four packages waiting for me thanks a million got everything from the lighter, pickles, peanut butter, 10 lbs. of candy 3 cartons of cigarettes + all. Thank all of you for all of your trouble.

I got a $103 on my Control book so I will send home much as possible when we can send money orders.

For the last 5 days all we did was ride, it took 2 days to get to Rheims so we picked up jeeps there + they asked for volunteers to go to Paris for trucks. I wouldn't go a damn bit further than I had to because it is cold over here.

On the way back we stopped in Metz France + Mannheim.

I would get so cold at times I would just sing + holler + try to keep warm.

I have pretty near got that T/4 sewed up they have got me down as a non-commissioned officer. I might as well make some money if I have to be in this army.

Slim expects to ship out soon then I will be lost. Just learned Whitey is in the guard house. I told you he got picked up in Munchen with a gun + they picked him up in Hiedenhiem after Curfew so I guess he will be hurting now.

March 9

Didn't do much today just made the company run + the chief took the CC"B" run.

They are getting awful chicken since we are going to the Constabulary force it is suppose to be the elite group of the army any how that is what the General said.

We are suppose to get all new clothes + look real sharp.

We have to take down all our pin-ups get rid of all bed, we are going to sleep on cots + a lot of little things like that are just going to make it a little less comfortable revile at 6:30 but Slim + I never fell out anyhow.

Us two are practically living like civilians any way.

Hope all of you people are alright.

March 9

Just been eating some of your crackers (+) peanut butter very good.

Didn't work today because I just got back yesterday.

Me+ Slim have a lot of trouble when we got the wash back. We try + separate it + argue which is whos.

What did you ever send the ribbons for? Slim is worried.

I will sign off now as there is no more to write + Slim wants to talk.

March 11, 1946

I am on C.Q. again tonight so I hope this will end up a long letter but seeing that I did not get any mail tonight it's hard to tell.

I've got over a hundred dollars so when I can I will send home a money order for the same amount as I have only got hundred + three dollars on my book.

When you do get it you can take what you need + deposit the rest if there is any to deposit. This stuff don't look like money but I guess it will be good to have a little when I get home. I hope to get there some day

That T/4 I was telling you about is in the bag. I am still driving but they are putting the constabulary into shape. I will have three up then + I will have to see if I can get any curving down.

I will be glad to get out of driving in a way. They are going to have 2 guys in Message Centre + I will be the second ranking guy so I will take it easy + there isn't anything to do anyway so I will have a racket. I will still hold the title of Code Clerk but I doubt if any code will ever come in but if it does I guess I can handle it alright. I am not going to worry about it anyway till it happens. I wish I had got in the armored force instead of infantry in the beginning. You cant make a darn thing in the infantry + you have got a chance here.

I was down to see Whitey in the Guard house yesterday+ took him some of your cigarettes + candy. He is up for a Special Courts Marshall + I believe he will get at least 6 months. You know he got picked up in Munchen with a foreign weapon + then got picked up in Heidenheim after curfew by the M.P. it was only 5 minutes past curfew but he is in for a god one anyhow. He was taking it pretty good any way+ said he never had it so good.

I don't feel sorry for him because he should have had better sense than doing what he did+ he never did care much what happened anyhow.

How is our little boy Carl making out?

I guess he will make out alright if he don't pop off to often especially in the States. Over here it doesn't matter so much you tell the first Sgt just the same as the pvt.

I've had two discussions with our company commander one about getting a day off a week that was when he said I was the only one to drive my jeep + then another time he wanted to break Slim + me up. They are not so bad if you talk right up to them.

Bob passive-aggressively suggests he might have free time during CQ to write a long letter, but since he's received nothing from home recently, it is unpredictable if he will write or not. So, if his family wants to hear from him, they'll need to send him a letter.

March 12

No mail again today somewhere along the line Good + proper.

We moved today just to another house just a couple of house(s) from the old place. Me + Slim swung a deal with the C.O. . . .

With the Calvary we have more guys in Message Centre than we know what to do with. I am still driving but it wont be for long + I will be glad to be finished.

This is kind of short but that is about all that is new for today.

Wednesday 13

Received the package with the underwear in it. Thanks a lot. Got here in good shape I haven't tried them on but I think they will be O.K.

I've got over 100 bucks[4] + over 100 worth of cigarettes so I guess you can let up on sending on cigarettes a bit.

We had to take out the beds today + we all got G.I. beds but they are pretty comfortable.

I sure am glad that I am in message centre because the line companies are starting to take basic training all over again + I never had it so good in the army as I have it now + wont do anything when I get relieved of driving a T four rating + T three rating in the army you have got that rank for you know not for what you do.

Ever since I got out of that 106 Division I've had it pretty easy. That was the most miserable time I ever spent any place.

That 3rd armored was alright too in the ration gang but this tops them all. Now if I can only stay in it.

. . . hope I get some mail tonight.

---

[4] $100 in 1946 dollars is worth approximately $1,400 in 2014 dollars, assuming four percent inflation per year.

March 14

Received another package last night + a couple of letters + a couple tonight from you + one from Carl.

I must have felt pretty low when I wrote you some letters I guess

Glad to hear Bud got home in some kind of good shape.

I was reading Butch's last night to Slim + Butch said do you hear Hop Harrigan + tonight I read another one where he asked me if I hear the Lone Ranger so Slim said that he was going (to) write that guy a letter he thought it was Carl all the time.

I guess I told you I got the underwear.

Bitching is complaining.

Hope daddy don't lose his job because I don't believe he will get a better one.

Sorry to hear the kids have been sick.

. . . (will) write to Carl.

Friday 16

Germany

Well here I am again trying to write you another letter.

I feel fine. We have been having fine weather just like July + August home.

Hope Butch + Janet are O.K. + and doing fine in school. What about sending the kids marks when they get them. I'll bet Daddy is still working nights. I hope you still have that letter from the Navy Yard because I read in the Stars+ Stripes where a lot of guys are having trouble about getting there old jobs back.

I got fifty dollars + pretty near two months pay coming.

We still didn't get any mail but that is because we have been

> *moving around so much.*
>
> *Give my regards to Charlie + his sister.*
>
> *You will probably get a letter from Willie one of the boys in the room. He thinks you wont answer him but I told him you would.*
>
> *They kid me about my big sister so have Janet write a letter to Isador Leo Grasso 42189950.*
>
> *Same address as mine.*
>
> *Well I'll sign off.*

> *March 17*
>
> *. . . received a letter from Gram Glover telling me about Frank Doroski getting married + that they are starting to plant potatoes.*
>
> *We are beginning to have pretty good weather + been real warm for a couple of days.*
>
> *Things look pretty bad with Russia. I wish they would wait till I get home at least.*
>
> *I am still waiting to get off driving+ and only work in the office. I wish they would get more guys because every time I mention it to the Commo. Officer he says the company is under strength.*
>
> *It sounds pretty good about two year men getting out in June. I hope they keep their word.*
>
> *I will get out next Dec anyhow.*
>
> *. . . I will . . . write to Gram Glover.*

It appears that Louise had her hands full caring for Butch and Janet, who were sick. To add to Louise's troubles, her mother in Greenport on the North Fork of Long Island was not well.

Trying to be sensitive to his mother's feelings, Bob was being a bit more positive in his letters.

March 19

. . . I used to go to Heidenheim in the evenings as you know but now I don't have to go there any more now that we are going to be cavalry + the Constabulary regt comes to us from Stuttgart so I have got it made now.

By the way you can start writing my mail A.P.O. 154 instead of 251 that will be our new A.P.O. but we have not changed the name of the outfit as yet.

We got a bunch of replacements in today but they were all re-enlisters. Most of them only for a year. Maybe I should have enlisted for a year a long time ago.

I put in for a $100 money order a long time ago so I'll maybe get it one of these days+ forward it to you.

You can do what you want with it.

Well I have been feeling kind of lazy the last couple of days because it has been real warm + plenty of sun shine.

Now that I have made out the $100 money order I have only $3.00 on my book + near $200.00 left so I will start to look around to see what I can buy real cheap that is worth something.

We read about no work + strikes all the time in the S+S so I don't know what to make of it. I don't think I will want to loaf too long when I got out. Maybe a couple of weeks then I want to go back.

How is Dad making out?

I have an Eversharp pen + pencil.

This is the pencil but I cant write with the pen so hot it has not got the right kind of point for me to write with.

Hope all of you people are alright + the kids are alright.

We cant have pin –ups anymore so I have Butch's picture framed. The one where he is in fatigues + by the water fountain.

I will sign off now with lots of love+ hope that I will be home soon+ we can get back to the old grind.

Washington DC faced a serious public relations problem following allegations that army personnel were profiting from black market trading in Germany.

In April 1946, Col. Francis P. Miller complained to the Public Health Service's Surgeon General, who was on a fact-finding tour of Europe. Miller was urged to take his concerns to a Senate special committee.

The following month, Miller testified in an executive session of the special committee. His testimony provided a graphic view of the "moral disintegration" of American officers and enlisted men in Germany. He added that American forces had become undisciplined, and cited how German citizens were accusing US soldiers of being "Russians with their trousers pressed."

Colonel Miller's testimony created a significant crisis for Washington politicians, who were already weary of dealing with the post-war cleanup. Republicans, eager to use scandals in the military government to attack the Truman administration, called for an immediate investigation.

In reaction to the news in Washington, military officials in Germany ensured that protocol was being followed as closely as possible. Hence, the order was given to remove all items that were considered immoral, including Bob's pinup posters.

March 20

Just received 3 letters from you people one from you + 2 from Butch.

Sorry to hear mail has been taking so long but it cant be helped. I guess yours was mailed the 4-12-13. That is pretty good I guess you cant complain to much.

Inclosed fined a $100.00 money order which is the most I can send home+ in my pocket I have $200.00 more which I expect to invest one of these days.

I got a G.I. Haircut today but it is still to long.

We are suppose to move very soon to Bamberg.

20 March 1946

From Pvt Carl Lange 42270550

3704 A.A.F. B. U. Sqd Z A 612

Keesler Field, Miss.

Dear "Mom"

Well, today I'm doing what I should have done about two months ago –that is to write to you.

I don't know what to write except that I miss you and the gram and the kids –I miss everybody.

Thanks very much for the Jelly Beans that you sent. You know just what I like. Speaking of things that I like I sure do miss your cooking. This army chow doesn't even come up to any of the dinners I ever ate at your house.

How are the kids behaving?

Do they still get on your nerves or have they quieted down a little.

Does Charlie still "assist" you in locating sugar + butter? In our mess halls we have plenty of each, but there's no way to send it, or else I would have sent some sugar long ago.

I cant think of much to write so I guess I'll have to close.

I hope your feeling good and don't have too much work to do.

Best regards,

Love,

Carl

In this letter, Carl goes on the offensive, writing directly to Louise in an effort to remain in the good graces of the family (despite Bob's comments).

March 21

. . . as I told you we are suppose to move to Bamberg that is right on the Russian Zone line. They say that there is nothing in the trouble with Russia that too many people are coming into the American zone. That is why we are going there.

I hope all of you people are feeling alright.

They was going to send me to constabulary school but I said I didn't want to go so that is that for this month but they said I might have to go for next month . . .

I played a little baseball today been pretty nice weather for the last week.

Sent the money order today so let me know if you get it.

I cant understand why you don't get mail I must write 5 days out of a week.

I don't know what I write but it(s) something.

> *You had better buy Butch + Janet something with the money order to make up for the helmets.*
>
> *Well I have eleven months overseas. I think it has gone by pretty fast.*

Following the end of the war, the Army needed to provide resources to manage both military and civilian populations. However, the primary objective at the time was the return of the US military forces to the United States. Many GIs wanted, and expected, to return home ASAP and were becoming frustrated and problematic to manage.

The Army was also faced with managing German citizens who were experiencing drastic changes in their lifestyle and habits. Germans had lived in a strict, regulated society for many years; in some areas mowing the lawn or shopping on Sundays had been prohibited—would these traditions be kept?

An additional concern for the Army was the fact that underground Nazis and criminals continued to scheme against the US troops. These concerns led the military to establish what the *Stars and Stripes* newspaper described as "Highly mobile mechanized security force units, which may prove more efficient for occupation duty than infantry-type troops, will be organized soon in occupied Germany on an experimental basis. Units, to be known as Constabulary, will specialize in patrolling and liaison with other control forces."

The plan was to form a police unit that used: armored cars, tanks, jeeps, motorcycles, and other vehicles outfitted with radio and signal equipment to allow for continuous contact with counter-intelligence corps, local military government officials, and German civilian police.

The US Constabulary had more power than the Military Police units; soldiers were initially selected from the 1st and 4th Armored Divisions to become members of this elite team. The

Constabulary headquarters was initially located in Bamberg in February 1946, and quickly recruited thirty-five thousand soldiers. It soon relocated to Heidelberg and on July 1, 1946, the Constabulary forces officially began to cover the US Zone of approximately forty-three thousand square miles where sixteen million Germans lived.

The Constabulary forces also had the responsibility of dealing with the Russian troops along the border, now numbering more than forty-five thousand. In time, the border was completely fenced off, but prior to that, the border was marked simply with red-tipped white poles and rocks.

Turnover of personnel became a key problem for the Constabulary; given the choice of staying in Germany or returning home to the United States, most soldiers opted to return home as soon as possible. In the first few months of operation, sixteen replacements were needed to fill the vacant Constabulary positions.

Bob saw this as an opportunity and investigated the Constabulary School, which provided the curriculum for a four-week course. Classes ranged from European/World politics to police patrol procedures.

The United States also relied on German police to assist them in patrols in cities and on the highways. The Constabulary and the German police were involved in many types of serious police activities; two examples from official reports are as follows:

"A large black-market ring which used two girls as lures to obtain gasoline from romancing US soldiers, was broken up by the arrests of 20 Germans in the vicinity of Aschaffenburg, US Constabulary headquarters disclosed. The girls lured soldiers with vehicles to their home and entertained them while confederates drained the vehicles of gasoline. Constabulary officials identified the leader of the ring as a clothing manufacturer, and estimated he had netted $60,000 from the ring's operations. They charged that the ring dealt in gasoline, jewels, clothing, typewriters, and sewing machines."

"Two Constabulary Troopers were killed near Hanau early today while trying to stop a speeding command car."

The Constabulary lasted for several years following the war. In December 1952 it was decided to cease operations and turn over all responsibilities to local police.

March 22

No mail again today. It has been cloudy all day today + looks like rain tonight.

Nothing much new today.

Played a little more ball + fooled around.

All I have to do now is to drive around the city here to the companies so I only go about 20 miles a day.

As I told you we are suppose to move to Bamberg soon.

I hope all of you people are O.K.

You don't tell me anymore about Jean is she working or what?

I guess Butch + Janet are the same as always.

Just about a yr ago we were on maneuvers + I remember being home on Easter + leaving the 7th of April + after that things went pretty fast. I hope next year at this time I am home.

March 24

Today is Sunday so we played ball from 8-11 this morning.

I don't think I'm as good as I used to be.

Time seems to be gone pretty fast it will be a year over here pretty soon.

There is not a darn thing to write about.

Had a flat tire today+ when I got the spare off it was flat too so I was in a fix.

Did I tell you what happened to Whitey? Well he had a hearing + got off with only a week's restriction, boy I call that lucky. He was AWOL, got caught with a concealed weapon + then broke restriction.

Went to Stuttgart yesterday to pick up some training film.

It was a nice ride because you go by Autobahn all the way so you can really go but there are some rough detours around some mountains. Most all the bridges are blown out.

It is nice riding on the Auto Bahn because it don't go through no towns + you can see a long ways in some places.

If they ever cut service down to 18 mos I'll have them because 1st of April I'll have 16.

3/25/46

Dear Doll,

Received a long letter from you tonight and I am on charge of quarters tonight so I guess this is good time as any to answer it.

First of all I write Mom pretty near every day. 5 out of 7 days a week and I do not know what happens to them if you do not get them.

There is nothing to write anyway but I try to write what happens etc.

And in the first place I was not made to be a writer.

I was all twisted up in the camera business. As you know I have another one now with a 7.7 lens. I guess it is not so hot.

Glad to hear you are going to be a stenotyper or whatever it is and hope you find a better job if you want a better one.

Guess Carl will make out alright in the army but I will have to keep jumping to keep ahead of him because they advance too fast in the air corp. I hope to make t/4 by June. I am doing the work now but I cannot make it until we are constabulary. Then I will be the I3 constabulary squadron code clerk.

I do not know about this coming home soon. I will have 16 months in the first of April but if they keep the two year service it will be a long time but if they ever cut it down to 18 months then I will have them where I want them.

I hear a lot of fellows are enlisting because they cant find work?

About this job business. I hope to go back to work at the navy yard and when that plays out try and go to plastic school or if I can go to plastic school after work. There must be something in the g.i. bill of rights about that. I never did care much about working inside. But maybe I will change.

We are suppose to move to Bamberg then to Bayreuth. That is right on the border of Russian occupation. They gave us a big speech on this . . . is not because the way the Russians are acting.

I will sign off now with love.

Love

Bob

Bob and his older sister Dolly had a good relationship, and typical of brothers and sisters, they bickered occasionally. However, they were both very family-oriented. Dolly had dated Carl for several years by this point and was likely frustrated and insulted by Bob's constant derogatory comments regarding Carl.

Dolly shot back at Bob by accusing him of not writing often enough. Bob tried to change the subject midway through his letter, instead writing about Dolly's training to be a stenotypist. As usual, Bob could not resist taking a poke at Carl and ended the letter by suggesting that the air corp advances and promotes men quicker then they deserve.

On the subject of Bob's promotion to T/4, he knew the paperwork had gone through successfully and now predicted he would be formally promoted in June.

∞∞ ∞∞ ∞∞

In late 1945 and 1946, there was great concern that the reduced demand for war materials would drive the United States economy back into the Great Depression. In addition, millions of soldiers—including Bob—were returning home and were looking for work. Congress hotly debated such economic issues as full employment and inflation, and they sought ways to preempt the anticipated problem.

The Employment Act of 1946 was designed to provide full-time employment for all Americans and assigned federal funds to achieve this goal. The bill needed to be passed quickly, as the economy dropped immediately after the end of the war, and returning veterans looking for work raised the unemployment rate to 7.9 percent in late 1949.

March 27

No mail again tonight.

I have been working on the jeep pretty near all day.

Now that I don't have to go to Heidenheim all I have to do is go to the companies+ they are all here in the city. I have it pretty easy now + when I am not working on the jeep I am in the red cross playing ping pong or eating donuts.

I have to go to Non- Commissioned Officers meeting Monday, Wednesday, + Friday from 7 P.M. to 9 so that kill(s) quite a few evenings.

Maybe you think I don't write much well I write more than I get that isn't a hint to write more because I realize things are not too easy for you home.

I have made up my mind to be a bum before re-enlisting. I am fed upon taking orders all the time.

Now that I am getting up in months of service (16) I at least feel better

I know that it cannot be too much longer.

I will sign off now + eat.

Bob's frustration continued to grow, as indicated by his cavalier attitude toward the NCO meetings and his comment about being "fed up." Adding to his frustration was his perception that things are "not too easy" at home for his mother, and he was not around to help.

March 29

We have had about a week straight of the best weather you could ask for + boy it makes me lazy + homesick. I remember a year ago when I was getting ready to come home.

I have got my heart + prayers set that they will cut it down to 18 months of service I hope they do. I have got it in me now that I have not got too much longer + I hope it is not.

I have to go to these meetings 3 nights a week now so that kills three nights a week.

> *I guess they have changed their minds about moving.*
>
> *Let me know if you have received the money order yet. I have over three hundred dollars now + cannot send it home.*
>
> *I will buy some jewelry or something.*
>
> *I bought a mechanical drawing set which is alright I guess.*

March 30ᵗʰ 1946

Addressed to: Miss Ruth Glover @ 599 W 178ᵗʰ Street)

Am sorry haven't answered your letter before this time, but I haven't written even home for a while as there isn't much to say. Your brother keeps on telling me, when are you going to write to my sister. The weather here is really nice cant wait to go swimming. Your brother is laying on the bed really the life. I'm sitting on Slim's bed writing this letter. I'm working in the kitchen now I mean putting in time. I was just telling your brother how much I eat. Ha Ha. I sure wish I was home this summer. I'm pretty sure I'll be home from Christmas. We went to Stuggart yesterday on business then went to a show at the Red Cross called The Spider Killing. Tell your Mother + Father I said hello + hope they are in the Best of health + feeling fine.

There really isn't much to say so maybe I'd better finish this letter. In the next letter I'll make it longer

As Ever

Whilden

P.S. Take good care of yourself

Pvt Wilmer R. Whilden 13201313
Hg. Co. 13ᵗʰ Tank Bn.
A.P.O. 154
C/o Postmaster, NY, NY

Bob convinced his Army buddy, Will, to write to Dolly in the hope that Dolly will become so infatuated with him that she would forget about Carl.

Easier said than done in this situation.

APRIL 1946—THE CIRCUS COMES TO ULM

April 3, 1946

Well mail has started to come again got 5 letters from you 1 from Janet + 1 from Butch. Well I shall start to answer them now.

I guess I do have my ups+ downs as you can tell by the letters.

You think it will be the happiest day in your life well it will be the happiest day for me too.

At least you gave me a heck of a lot of encouragement of coming home with those clippings of the jobs. I hope I make get a good job when I get out.

You said you didn't know what I mean by saying when I got back there was four packages waiting when I got back from France.

As you know Whitey is out now + working in the kitchen he brings me sandwiches all day long. He is a good natured kid but don't seem to use his head much or he don't care.

If you get time write him a letter he don't get much mail.

I got the underwear alright but the pants are too big. 30 or 32 fits good not 34.

I know it costs like heck but if you can afford it get a couple more T shirts. I wear 2 and Slim wears 1. You got the right size shirt even if the shoulders stick out an inch past where they are suppose to.

Glad to hear Carl is getting along alright.

Don't worry about me getting in the guard house. I try to control myself.

If I ever get broke don't worry about it I don't care what I get home a Pvt or sergeant.

I don't believe I was made to be controlled like a guy is in the army. When I was home I was quiet but at work I told them what I thought + I still do the same.

Too bad dad don't have much work.

Glad to hear you are sending more packages + I read the funnies.

While I think of it you might as well send mail 3 cents it comes just as quick.

Don't worry about re-enlisting.

Don't worry about re-enlisting.

Don't worry about us guys we are alright + will always be.

Glad to hear you have been taking pictures I have got one of you taken in 1940.

2 of our companies have a case of measles so they both are restricted.

Hope you can cash the stamps.

I will send I will get fifty dollars' worth tomorrow + I will order some more.

Black marketeering seemed to be going well for Bob. His request for fifty dollars' worth of stamps suggests that stamps were also a marketable currency, almost as valuable as dollars. Stamps were now being used as an alternative form of money—a creative solution to the Army's efforts to control currency. Soldiers were not required to include the dollar value of stamps in their currency control books. Bob was becoming a skilled entrepreneur.

April 2

No mail in quite a while now + some of the fellows have been getting telegrams from their wives that they have not got any mail in 3 weeks + these guys claim to write pretty near every day. All I can do is write + and if they don't get there I don't know what happens to them. Just do not worry because I write often as I can. I missed a couple of days because we have not got mail in so long.

I have been running into a little trouble with the company commander over the jeep so I might be busted any day it don't mean nothing to me except the pay

I got paid yesterday $54 so I will send that much home when we can make out money orders.

I ordered fifty dollars' worth of stamps. I hope you can cash them or something if you cant hold on to them + some day they might come in handy.

. . . I put in for a fifty five dollar money order + will get it in a couple of days. That is as much as I can send.

I just got back from Stuttgart again they tell me at 4 o'clock that I have to go + then I just got back now at 9. It is about 100 miles round trip + I stopped at the Red Cross in Stuttgart + on the autobahn coming + going so that was not too bad.

Boy I cannot wait till I get out of this army now + it cant be too quick.

That will be a great day when I am a free man again.

They are getting to be real strict again + the line companies are taking training. I work all day finish at 4:30 get ready for a retreat at 5:30 +eat + at 6:30 on 3 nights a week go to school from 7-9 + one night every 2 weeks pull C.Q.

I will sign off now + it wont be to much longer.

April 5

No mail today except a letter from Carl. He seems to sound pretty happy anyhow. Maybe that is because he thinks he is not going overseas.

I sent about 12 letters with stamps in them today it was $40 dollars' worth or more. I hope you can cash them if you want to.

Had to go to Stuttgart again today + I just got finished + it is after 9 o'clock.

I got stopped by a colonel on the autobahn for having 3 in the front + he took our names so maybe that will be the end of me as a non-com but if he sends the report through message center it will get lost by accident.

April 9

Received a letter from you of April 1 + a package of Feb 20.

Last couple of days I have not been feeling so good. I got a cold + feel lousy.

Do not worry about me enlisting anymore I wouldn't for nothing I cant wait till I get home.

You should have one money order pretty near $50 worth of stamps. I got another money order coming for $55.

All I got on my mind now is coming home.

Things look pretty good as far as service + time goes for discharge.

This is pretty short but this is it. Thanks for the packages.

April 10 Postmarked US Army Postal Service

Received an Easter Card from Dolly tonight. I am always glad to hear from my sister.

I sent another money order today for 55 dollars. Hope you are getting all of these alright.

Glad to hear that all of the kids are feeling good. Hope daddy keeps on working + keeps well.

You are about the only one that I write to now although I write to other people but only on special occasions.

This afternoon the whole company including the colonel went + played ball but I had to stay in the office.

They think the constabulary is going to be a great thing+ it is getting to be awful strict on everything. That is what is making me want to get home all the faster. I think I would be a bum before I enlist.

I feel better today I guess all I have got is a cold.

They gave us another speech tonight on the condition the states is in.

April 12 1946

No mail yesterday . . .

I have got a mechanical drawing set so I will see if I can get a box made. These Heinies are getting too independent.

Where you used to give them a few cigarettes they want a pack now. You then get into an argument with them and you finally do not get anything done

Every day I get more discussed with things in general. I guess it is the life you lead over here it is the same thing day after day

Ha-ha-ha-ha-ha the bell rang.

In the previous letter, Bob explored the various trades he could learn while waiting to be sent home. The fact that he actually acquired a mechanical drawing set and told his family about it was a positive step forward.

The concept of using cigarettes as currency was short-lived in Germany in 1946. During this time, a GI could sell most of his month's ration of cigarettes for German marks, then trade in the marks for dollars at a profitable, fixed exchange rate.

The black market was booming; cigarettes, chocolate, liquor, and food were the most easily disposable commodities that soldiers could trade. Cigarettes were a good example of the profit that could be made; American soldiers could buy ten packs of cigarettes for fifty cents each at the PX and then sell them for up to one hundred dollars each. Bob's continued requests for watches and cameras were not surprising, as they were among the most lucrative items on the black market.

The Russians were considered to be the key drivers of the black market. Russian soldiers had a huge appetite for watches, associating them with affluence. Also, because Russian troops had little confidence in their own currency, they invested in alternate items of value like expensive watches.

With the Allies' blessing, the Soviets had printed huge amounts of "occupation currency" to pay their troops, who had served for years without compensation. The soldiers went on a black market spending spree in 1945; they had to spend the occupation currency in Germany, as it would not be allowed to be taken back to the USSR.

April 12 evening

On these spring evenings I get more home sick than usual. Maybe I was too much of a home boy when I was home. As I sit here in the room alone I can recall many an evening with just the same kind of weather home. Pitching horseshoes or just sitting with you. I guess everything like that you remember maybe next "year"? I will remember just how I feel now. I remember when I used to go by the Harlem River in the eve + sit + think + watch the trains go by. It used to be so quiet by there + nobody would bother you. Someday I hope to go + sit there again + just sit + smoke till I get chilly then go home.

A person does not appreciate home till he is away from it.

By the way I received a letter from you tonight of the April 4.

Glad to hear you got the money order alright you should get another one + about $50 worth of stamps.

What will I do if + when I get home? Go back to Navy Yard? Always good working for Govt? Get another job? Take up plastics? I never did get them out of my head.

I think I should go right back to work for the Navy Yard + take up plastics at night if I could. If not still go back to work for the Navy Yard. I always liked sheet metal. I get a kick out of making things + making the patterns so it comes out right.

You feel great when you do a good job making something like that.

I finished half of my apprentice ship so I might as well complete it.

There are only two things you want out of life as I figure it that is stay healthy + live comfortably + everything else will fall in with those things.

. . .

Homesick Bob

P.S. Don't wait for no new address to send packages! Bestampt

April 15

No mail in the last couple of days

We haven't had any rain in so long it is not funny. I guess when we do get it we will get it for a long time . . . every day I pray that they will cut it down to 18 mos of service.

The first of June I would have 18 mo but it would still take a long time after they cut it down.

A year ago today we left New York Whitey is one of the few who came with me + are still together there are about 5 in the company.

I hope that I come home quick.

April 19

Received 3 Easter cards tonight two from you + the other one from Dad.

I read in the Stars + Stripes where you cannot cash those stamps so it will save you the money of buying them.

Nothing new around here same old stuff. Been raining on + off yesterday + today.

Time seems to be going by pretty fast. Last year at this time I was coming over.

Here are some more pictures.

Things look pretty good according to the papers. That is about getting out.

P.S. Send more film.

April 23, 1946

I received a letter yesterday + one today + Whitey also got one.

I feel a little down in the dumps today just feel low.

Glad to hear you got the stamps even if you cant cash them. You can use them to send mail to me.

Received your colored pictures all of you look pretty good. Send some more. You look just as good as ever.

I have got 3 handkerchiefs made in Switzerland cost quite a bit but I might as well spend the money. I'll send them in separate envelopes.

Enclosed are the pictures I took but most of them are printed on rotten paper.

Hope all of you are feeling alright so I will sign off as I do not feel so hot.

April 26

Did not receive any letters yesterday but got two packages both with a carton of cigarettes + one with 4 rolls of film. Well thanks a lot for all of it + I will send some more pictures home when I get some.

The Krauts have been stealing in our house like hell. If I ever catch one he will wish he never started.

Slim didn't come home yet. It is hard to get in these hospitals but once you get in it is just as hard to get out.

Me + Whitey went to the club last night. The other night we went to a small circus they are having down here for a couple of days + naturally we sit way in the back + laugh our heads off.

A big elephant come out + did all kinds of tricks then he picked up the girl in its trunk + started off on three legs + about that time he decided he had to take a crap so he did and one of the guys there jumped up + tried to push his tail down. Laugh thought I would die.

By the way your packages were mailed March 19+22.

It is cold as the devil in the morning + then at noon it gets awful hot.

Got some more information on Weimar it is nearer Heilbronn than Stuttgart + they say it is a famous old town + has the Statue of Schiller there. If I ever get a chance, I will get a picture of it.

April 24

I didn't get any mail tonight. Didn't do much all day. I don't remember if I told you or not but Slim went to the hospital Monday with tonsillitis so I went to Stuttgart to see him this afternoon + when I got there he was in a show. He is a lot better but says he wont get out for 3 or four more days.

Sent 3 handkerchiefs yesterday. Hope you receive them.

It will be another month gone by pretty soon + I will get another money order off soon as possible.

We got 75 more replacements in the Battalion today.

Now we got 1 E. T. Jacket + two blouse they are trying to shape us all up for this constabulary.

We are suppose to get suntan shirts + more pants. I got my E.T. Jacket cut down + it fits me like a glove now.

April 27th 1946
Ulm, Germany

Dear Mrs. Glover

I received a letter from you yesterday + I was glad to receive the letter. You mentioned that Bob + I must be having a good time, we are. We came over on the same boat together + I hope we go home on the same boat. I'm not very good on writing letters I usually go on one question to another. Ha Ha.

This Weither really makes me homesick at times.

Bob is sleeping right now, he usually takes a nap after dinner, it is pretty hard for me to sleep during the day. I guess he told you I was working in the kitchen or I mean putting in time. Ha Ha.

I guess he told you Slim went to the Hospital. Had a sore throat, he's in Stuttgart. Bob + I went to see him the other day, he's ok now just waiting for them to discharge him from the hospital.

We had some more pictures taken the other day sure hope they come out. You know Mrs. Glover there is not a better fellow I'd rather of met than bob he is a really swell guy + Slim the same.

Tell Mr. Glover + Ruth I said hello + hope they are in the Best of Health + feeling fine.

I bet New York is really hot a lot of people will be going to the shore I guess. You know its only 2 hours ride from my home to yours.

Bob showed me the pictures you sent of you + his kid sister + brother there really good.

The first boatload of (don't know how to spell that word) should of finished school. Ha Ha.

Soldiers wives arrive tomorrow, they are supposed to arrive the 28th of April. I told bob my mother is getting a new car 46 Lincoln Convertible, cant wait until I get home + drive it. There really some pretty songs coming over the radio now.

I'll close now, Take good care of yourself+ give Mr. Glover + Ruth my best wishes

All my love,

Whitey.

P.S. Take it Easy

April 28

Well here it is another Sunday again time is moving right along.

No letters or packages yesterday.

Ma, how about a hair brush?

If you can find one.

How about looking up the description of Ichibog (Ichabod) Crane in Sleepy Hollow + sending it to me.

I got another letter from Slim + he wants me to come see him again but it is too far.

Good rumors about going home going around again. I hope it will be soon. I do not know how it is for jobs + so on but you can collect $20 a week if you don't work + I know that I would be better off all the way around home.

April 30

....stars+ Stripes say mail is suppose to get here in 4 -7 days now.

I entered Jeanie's + Dollie's pictures in a beauty contest at the Red Cross. If they come in first, the Red Cross is suppose to send them some flowers.

Slim was suppose to come home yesterday but he didn't so I called him up + said he would be back today for sure.

Put a roll of film in the foto shop today + they will be ready next Monday.

We are scheduled for a move this month to Breyruth near Bamberg

We are to become semi-operational this month and full operational the first of June.

Is Daddy still working at the Navy Yard?

234

MAY 1946—SERGEANT T/4

May 5

No mail in about a week.

We have been having pretty good weather + have had a couple of thunderstorms.

Slim finally got back out of the hospital.

Well I made the T/4 get the same pay as a buck sergeant.

Didn't send any money order this month, they give you a half a day to get them in + if you don't make it you have to wait another month.

Everything is constabulary they are going to have the jeeps all painted up + helmets + everything else they throw a constabulary insignia.

There isn't nothing new except I am mailing home a camera + a watch. I don't know if it will get there or not but I will try it anyway. The camera cost $1.70 in the P.X. + the watch I bought for $25 off a Kraut.

P.S. Send a package "tuna fish"?

May 6

Received a long letter + a four word letter tonight also one from Gram Glover + an Easter Card from Mrs. Newsom.

Been working quite a bit last few days getting the jeeps ready to paint + so on. They also say we are going to move again pretty soon.

There is no kidding this constabulary is going to be a sharp outfit.

I never got a letter from Felix.

> *I never sent no money order this month. Just was not there at the right time to make one out.*
>
> *Slim's father is in the hospital with heart trouble he is worried . . .*
>
> *I feel kind of funny being called sergeant + get an awful ribbing sometimes I wish I didn't make it. You got to be a hell sometimes + before I lose some friends they can have it back.*
>
> *Whitey is just as crazy as ever + has got blood poisoning in his hand. He is just like Teddy Doroski only more crazier.*
>
> *I am sending some negatives you can get them printed this paper isn't any good.*

Whitey was fortunate that he did not get his infection a few months earlier. During the 1940s all infections were considered serious, especially blood infections. The introduction of penicillin is recognized as one of the greatest advancements in medicine, particularly as an effective tool to fight infections. Before the introduction of penicillin, hospitals were crowded with patients who had gotten infections from as little as a simple cut, and doctors had virtually nothing to help. During World War II, penicillin, considered the first of the "wonder drugs," was considered so valuable to the war effort that the United States decided to support production on a commercial scale. In March 1944, with US government support, Pfizer opened in New York the first manufacturing plant to produce the drug.

During the war, the United States Army realized the benefits of penicillin in treating surgical and wound infections, and it was also discovered to be effective against syphilis. It became the primary treatment in the British and American armed forces. Whitey was as lucky as he was crazy.

7 May 1946

On Squadron M Letterhead. Chanute Field- Ill.

Dear Janet,

I got a letter from Dolly today and she told me that you were confirmed a few days ago. Congratulations, honey.

You already know where I am now and I think you would like it here. There's lots of open space and you can see for miles and miles.

I'm going to school now just like you and I have to study and do homework. We get about 1 test every day. If you don't pass you really have to work. It's worse than grade school.

I have a test to study for so I'll have to end this letter.

Love,

Carl

Carl's letter to Janet is another example of Carl's attempts to endear himself to the other members of the Glover family.

May 8

Just dropping you a short line.

Today is a holiday + all we had was a talk by the chaplain + the Bn. C.O.

It has been raining all day pretty hard.

Wrote a letter to Gram + Pop Glover today.

Slim + Whitey have gone to the club + I am home all alone.

They say when we go to Bayreuth we are going to live outside. Now that is crazy it gets pretty cold nights.

How are the kids + the rest of the family?

May 9, 1946

Ulm Germany

Well here I go again trying to write you another letter. I received 3 Easter Cards today+ I am also on C.Q. tonight which is bad.

Since I have made Sgt they are trying to get me off of driving but I am going to stick as long as possible.

Slim, Whitey + I went to the club last night+ they got kidding me about being Sgt + I got so mad I tore my stripes off. I think I will be lost when Slim leaves. He will have 2 yrs in August but he is a good kid + deserves to go home.

We are having good weather I remember last year it was much colder.

I have not heard anything about the 18 months of service while you are still a teenager. Well it probably wont be much over another 6 months anyway they put it.

The Colonel's wife is suppose to be here in 2 weeks, he is the only one so far that I know of whos family is coming over

I didn't write to Jean yet I don't think + while I am on that subject neither Jean not Doll won the beauty contest very disappointing.

I was going to send you a telegram but I thought maybe you would get all excited for nothing.

May 15, 1946

Received a letter from you + one from Gram Macomber . . .

Glad to hear you mailed a hairbrush. I need one every once in a while. I get mad + get a crew cut.

Don't bother to send any pencils I can get all the pencils I need.

Glad to hear you got a kick out of that elephant we still laugh at it. The Red Cross women left for another place maybe she was too embarrassed

I feel pretty good now + had the same thing I had a year ago. All I did for 3 days when I was sick was get up + get out for inspections + after inspection I would go back to bed.

Had a short circuit in my jeep so I went to a hienie shop to get it fixed + I got sick for the Old Navy Yard. I seen those guys working.

I don't believe it will be too hard to go back to work.

Well it don't look as if I will get out till next Dec now that they are discontinuing the draft. I guess it don't make much difference though.

May 17

. . . didn't write any last night as I went to Stuttgart + didn't get back until midnight.

I sent the camera today by airmail I don't know how much it cost yet but it cant cost too much.

I am suppose to get some pictures tomorrow from the shop + I will send them home.

I read where they are going to continue the 2 year of service till the end of June. I hope they cut it down then.

Today I was in another heinie shop + I feel right at home in a shop like that

I have also been reading some on Plastics. I don't think I would like it. It is too, well I cant explain it. Well any way it takes too many operations to make a thing + all a fellow does is one operation like operating a press or casting but there are some good angles like a die maker but I would have to start off again *as an apprentice to get anywhere.*

The composition of plastics would take a couple of years of Chemistry. It sounds simple to say it is made out of vegetables or animal matter but there are all kinds of chemicals added.

I think I will stick to sheet metal I like it + maybe I could get somewhere.

One thing sure I could never work in an office for a living because I cant sit still long enough.

I will sign off now as it is 11 o'clock.

May 20

Received 3 letters tonight all mailed May 14. All short.

You said you were glad to hear I had advanced well that's as far as I will ever get. In this army that's the way they work.

Now I have got a good racket.

Don't do nothing but drive + don't pull no Guard on C.Q. once every 2 or 3 weeks.

It has been awfully hot today just like July

Went to Augsburg yesterday. I took one of the fellows to see his cousin.

I think before I get out I will have at least 5 yrs in the army.

Sorry to hear Dad is going to be laid off.

Bob's father Roy worked several types of construction jobs between the 1940s and 1960s, and was adept at finding new work as a carpenter or a steel worker on projects in the New York City area. Similar to other industries, the job market in the construction industry fluctuated with alternating boom and bust times for commercial and residential projects.

In the 1950s, Roy landed a job on the project to build the Governor Malcolm Wilson Tappan Zee Bridge, an exciting new bridge that would connect the east and west sides of the Hudson River a half hour north of New York City. It would be New York State's largest bridge and would span the river almost at its widest point.

The job went well for Roy until the structure began to reach beyond the banks and extended over the deep waters of the Hudson River. At this advanced stage of construction, the story goes that Roy looked down from his workspace, saw the rushing waters of the Hudson far below, and discovered that he was afraid of heights. He immediately chose to find other means of employment.

May 21

Just got back from seeing the picture Gertie's Garter (pretty good). It is a quarter to 10 so this will probably be a short one.

No mail tonight.

Mom there is nothing to write. We do the same thing over + over.

I try to write you a letter+ I get all twisted up + I must write the same thing in every one.

I sent the camera + watch by air mail. You might say they didn't cost nothing so if you can (get) $10 or $15 out of them go ahead. The camera cost me $1.78 + the watch $25 (Black market). They are coming air mail so I guess it will get there.

What is Dad going to do now?

This month seems to be dragging.

May 23

No mail today. Been raining on + off today. We have been getting

---

> *quite a bit lately.*
>
> *Time is dragging lately I guess I think about it too much.*
>
> *I have been having trouble with my jeep lately. It wont start good + isn't running right*
>
> *Is Dolly still working for contact lens?*
>
> *There is not nothing to write I try to think of things + I write them as they come.*
>
> *The Sqdn is still way under strength + 250 expect to leave next month + you see very few fellows who just came over. If they don't continue the draft + keep discharging guys with 2 yrs the whole thing will fall apart. They will have to continue the draft or keep guys in longer*
>
> *I will sign off now+ maybe next time I will have something to write about.*

Bob's concern was that the squadron was undermanned, which could lead to safety issues, and it could also affect the Army's decision to keep soldiers like Bob in Germany for longer periods of time.

> *May 24*
>
> *Well another month is pretty nearby + I am getting closer to getting home.*
>
> *They issued us yellow scarfs today. I guess they are going to try + decorate us all up.*
>
> *A hundred replacements suppose to come in tomorrow. Maybe I will get to come home yet. These guys that are coming are suppose to be all regular army guys.*
>
> *No mail today the days are getting long over here it is day light till about 9:30.*
>
> *There is not a darn thing to write about.*

Bob received his bright yellow scarf, designed to highlight and identify the Constabulary troopers. The rest of his uniform included combat boots with a smooth outer surface and a helmet with the Constabulary insignia and yellow-and-blue stripes. The "lightning bolt" shoulder patch had a combination of yellow, blue, and red colors to represent the cavalry, the infantry, and artillery.

May 27 Eve.

Well here we start off on the evening session I received one letter today with a picture of Felix in it postmarked the 20th.

I am no more a jeep driver so I guess I will have to stay in the office. Maybe I'll be sorry I ever made T/4.

Glad to hear you are mailing (unintelligible) packages.

I was suppose to go to a meeting tonight but didn't go.

I am eating some of the candy you sent me (Nut Caramel Assortment)

Slim expect(s) to leave next month. They are sending or starting to send guys home a couple of months ahead of time so maybe I will get home in October or sometime around there. I don't believe there is any more hope for the 18 months of service. Whitey come in the army the same day as me so I guess we will go home together.

May 28

Received a letter today which was written simultaneously (mean same time) by carl+ Felix Swaitochia pretty good!?

No mail from you today.

Well since I am not driving anymore I don't do nothing except write a few things in a book+ Go to the Red Cross.

Just took a shower. It was pretty nice today + this morning the whole company had to go out + fire the machine gun for like so you wont forget how it works.

I am on C.Q. tomorrow night so you will most likely get a letter.

They are shipping guys out 2 months ahead of there 2 years so maybe I'll start on my way in October. I hope.

It is bound to happen one of these days. (I cant get home too quick+yet I don't know? I guess it will be good to do + go where you want for a change.

I am in a low mood now there is not a day that goes by without talking for a couple of hours on home.

I will sign off now so I can go to bed. I hope all of you are feeling good + well+ hope to see all of you soon. We will sit in the kitchen + make fun of the neighbors.

May 31

Received a letter tonight from Doll tonight + will answer it after this.

Bad or Good news either way want to say. Quite a few boys are going home including Slim + two other boys out of this house. So I don't feel so good. One of these days in the future I might get started I guess it will be at least another 3 months before I even start. But it probably will go by fast.

I hope that I get home + long as it is not too long I guess it will be alright

I guess that is about all for today. It was a pretty good day with a little rain.

JUNE 1946—CONSTABULARY TRAINING

June 1, 1946

Nothing much new today. I received a letter from Butch saying you got the camera. It isn't much good but it is worth a couple of bucks I guess.

We are having more rain over here every day it rains all day or half a –day.

I feel pretty low since a lot of the boys are leaving. Especially Slim we have lived together for 7 months + have had some good times together it is just as if I was leaving home again instead of him going home. There could not be a better guy. Someday I am going to Kentucky to see him. Keep this address

> *K.R. Foster*
> *923 East Washington St.*
> *Louisville, Ky.*

I believe this is the worst part of the army because you are always leaving friends.

They say all the fellows who are not regular army will be out of const by the last of June. I don't give a darn now because I am just going to coast the rest of the way through this army + going to do the least as possible.

I am going to have to start driving again. There is suppose to be 9 fellows in M/C + now there will only be 2 of us.

I have been thinking I have only been home 10 days out of 18 months. That isn't much is it?

Bob referred to his time spent on the Hudson River and in Staten Island, waiting with his unit to be shipped out to Europe.

June 2, 1946

Nothing much new rained all day today.

I will be glad when Slim + the rest of these guys leave because maybe I'll feel better then. They are suppose to leave Tues. right now I feel like two cents I guess I am home sick. When these guys leave I will probably be alright till the next bunch ship out. These guys are leaving me a lot of stuff like field jackets, pants, underwear, everything.

I will get a hundred dollar money order made out tomorrow or the next day.

I would never re-enlist in this army but what will happen when I get home.

You might say "What next Glover". We will find out in three or four months anyway.

Have you seen Bud yet?

Whats up home is Daddy through with the Navy yard?

I don't believe I wrote Gram Glover or Gram Mac in a long time . . .

You can send a package if you want never did get the hair brush.

June 3, 1946

I got a box + a letter tonight thanks a lot the box had a May 9th paper in it + also had the hair brush + cigarettes + candy thanks a lot for it all.

Everything is in a turmoil here

Slim + two other fellows leave from this house tomorrow + that only leaves two of us in the house.

They are giving me clothes left + right I got about 4 field jackets 10 pair of pants + shirts + plenty of underwear + socks. So don't send any more of that stuff.

I feel pretty bad with these guys leaving they were always fooling around+ right in the gang. The three wrote out a statement that I could have there packages if any come.

Your letter was dated the 21 May

Glad to hear you got the package

That watch cost 2 carton of cigarettes + I got robbed at that the camera cost $1.78 in the P.X. I have a darn good 15 Jewel Swiss watch that I got in the P.X. on. Keeps perfect time.

The one that I bought in the navy yard is messed up a bit so I will send it home I think it is still usable. See what you can get for that watch I sent.

I do get more money now. I get $96 a month but I am not going to make out any allotment or more bonds. I could pretty definitely promise you I will be home for good in Sept if they keep sending home like they are. Sounds good doesn't it.

These fellows with 21 months of service when they leave are on the boat in a week or less.

I will have 21 months the first of Sept + and they are shipping these guys out of this constabulary who are not regular army + they don't seem to want them anywhere else. Most of the fellows here have 18 months like me except some who came over last Dec.

Don't get your hopes too high but . . . all men are supposed to be out of here (I mean the cost) by the last of June. And if —they don't want us anywhere else?? What happens?

Now don't get feeling too good I may be here next year at this time.

I feel lost now with the fellows going home. I will have to work pretty much as there will only be two of us.
I will write more tomorrow

June 5, 1946

Didn't receive any mail yesterday or today.

Slim + the boys left yesterday so everything is pretty quiet around. Me+ Joe the guy left in the house had to move today because we were the only fellows in the house+ I guess they wanted to give it back to the krauts.

I was elected (as) one of the boys to go to Boblingen last night to listen to a Col talk. The way he talked things don't look so hot for the army. He was a good talker+ talked for an hour but we had to go past Stuttgart about 65 miles.

They are collecting all the men with children + are going to ship them home.

All of the fellows are "bitching" some of these guys only been in the army 8 or 9 months + now they get out. I guess you had better not plan on seeing me in Sept because Oct sounds more like it now.

I don't miss Slim as much as I thought I would. I guess I have got used to it in the army. He was a good egg + probably will never see him again. You are always making + losing friends in the army.

Tomorrow is a holiday being that is D-day a couple of years ago.

We got to talking about how much we weighed today + they say I weigh between 180-190.

I don't believe it.

The way this army fools you around you get so mad sometimes you feel like re-enlisting.

I was talking to a fellow who had re-enlisted after he was discharged + he said it isn't the army you miss but the fellows + you don't come back to the same fellows.

If Slim ever decides to join again he is going to write me + see how I am making out.

I got a hundred dollars to send home but I don't know if I will get around to making one out.

June 13, 1946

Did not write in the last couple of days as there is nothing new.

This month is going by pretty fast. I guess that is because I try + push it. We got a package from Slim's mother see he had willed them to me + another guy.

Right now it is raining like the devil out + does not look like it is going to stop.

What ever happened to Arthur did he come over again or not?

This army gets to be a bore after a while you do the same thing day after day.

We are suppose to move the twenty first of this month to Bayreuth. I guess this time we will move for sure as the fellows will be finished training then + we are suppose to become operational.

The boys are not doing bad right now. The Krauts + the other soldiers call the constabulary boys S.S. boys + Gestapo. It will be a good outfit + you shall hear about it. It has all kind of priorities for everything + they are trying to make soldiers out of the boys again. We got about one hundred young kids that had signed up for three years. Will they be sorry? Most of them don't look like they could hold a job so it does not worry me. So that paper for the Navy yard job still good.

One thing for sure I do not believe I shall ever work on a farm again. I remember those guys saying after the work a lot of guys would be back picking potatoes. Well here is one boy who is not

> *going to pick potatoes.*
>
> *I'll clean the street first.*
>
> *Some time you don't have nothing to do see what it will cost to go to a plastic school + what requirements you have to have. I could probably get the school free but about how much would it cost and give me a total on what money I have?*
>
> *I want to get settled what I am going to do when I get home. It will not be too much longer + I would like to get that straight. What I am planning on is getting something with a job to keep. The Navy Yard might fold up. Don't say it wont because if the navy has fell apart like the army they wont have nothing to do. I could get a job over here as a civilian at twenty five hundred or less or more but I want to get home. Let me know what you find out + everything will get settled. I got it in my head I will be home before long. I probably will. I hope so.*
>
> *I will write more tonight as I am on C.Q.*

There were several recorded examples of the members of the Constabulary abusing their authority; unfortunately, to civilians, this aggressive behavior was reminiscent of the SS and the Gestapo—two infamous Nazi organizations noted for their cruelty.

Bob continued to ponder his life and career beyond the Army. Growing up on a farm during the Great Depression left its mark on Bob. He vowed that he would never again return to farming; in fact, his whole family had vowed they never would return. It was often a painful subject for the family to discuss.

> *June 14, 1946*
> *Dear Dad,*
> *I received your letter tonight and was glad to hear from you. It has been quite a while since I wrote or received a letter from you.*

I guess I will be able to find a job when I get home. Most of these guys that re-enlist come from the hills. I guess they never worked anyway. They are the laziest bunch of guys I ever seen. One thing is there are three of them in the office + they treat me like a king. The let me sit in front of the jeep as if I wouldn't tell them to get in the back.

In a lot of ways they show it.

All I got on my mind is getting out + staying out. There is nothing much to do now but just the same I don't like it. I guess it is just because it is the army.

I don't even plan on getting anywhere near $2.00 per when I get home that sounds too good+ don't forget I am not a first class mechanic.

That wrist watch I (sent) you isn't so hot but I have got a "prema" on now that cost $42 off the book.

I guess everything is about the same home. I feel as good as ever but I think I am getting lazy.

I will close now as that is all there is to write.

Watch for write ups about constabulary in the paper. We go operation (al) 1 July or earlier

Love

Bob

June 15, 1946 (in pencil)

Just received your letter of the 10th very good time.

You said Daddy had a job. Well that made me curious as you said you would tell me more if he stuck to it. What kind of a job is it? + what is he pulling down a week? You left me in suspense.

It has cleared up here today for the first time in quite a while but it does not look as if it is going to stay.

We are moving next Friday to Bayreuth it is not too far from Bamberg. We sure have been in Ulm long enough. Since the first part of December I guess.

June 16, 1946

Well Dad I have write to pretty near everybody else today so I might as well make it complete. The only reason I am writing it is Sunday and it is raining and I do not feel like sleeping. This will probably be dull but I will try it. They shipped out last night all the fathers that wanted to go back to the states. That is all of them no matter how long they have been in the army. Some of them had only been over here a couple of months. I call that a big break you might say they just came over to see what it looks like here. I was pretty discussed when I first heard it but I guess it is alright because I do not believe it will interfere with my departure. This is a funny army it is falling apart from lack of men and yet they keep sending the fellows home. They will come to their senses one of these days and stop everybody that is going home. It is a shame but fellows like me that expect to go home in the near future do not care but they will not have control with a couple of thousand men and they will run in to all kind of trouble.

I mean that I cannot see that and honest I hate to see these Krauts take over right now. At the end of the war they got off the sidewalk but now some of them now try to make you move off. And to go out at night is taking your life in your own hands. The d.p. are as bad as the Krauts. They sit around all day and eat the food that comes from the states and at night they go look for trouble. They most generally find it because a G.I. is just like a sailor he never lets a fight go by.

I don't know what is going to happen but all I care is that I will soon get out of here.

I want to talk something over with you. A fellow can save a lot of money over here. Whatever you get paid is a clear savings because you can get by on selling a couple of cartons of cigarettes a month. What do you think of re-enlisting I am almost positive that I could make T/sgt in a couple of months and with that rating you pull down about one hundred and thirty a month. Boy you would have to work like hell to make anywhere near that in the states. Just give me an honest answer and do not tell me to decide for myself because that is a big question and it will probably decide my whole future. Well write back and let me know what you think and I will think it over in the meantime. Do not get all excited over it just think it over a couple of days and then let me know. I certainly do not like it over here but I am trying to see ahead a little.

Mom said you had a job but did not say what kind, she said she would see if you stuck to it then let me know. Well what about telling me?

I guess that is all for now and do not forget and let me know what you think.

LOVE

BOB

It is clear from Bob's letter that the Army was having a difficult time balancing the needs in Europe versus the need to send solders home as soon as possible.

The original "point plan" establishing the eighty-five points the amount needed to be sent back to the States had become extremely unpopular with the enlisted men, and many demanded to return home immediately. After additional consideration, the Army decided to prioritize the return home of soldiers with children.

Bob understood that this was necessary, but he also saw firsthand the gaps in resources caused by the men going home. He knew that the Army could not maintain control over Europe with only a few thousand men, but where were the new men to come from?

In addition, German citizens had become frustrated with the American soldiers who had taken up residence in their communities. Bob suggests that the displaced persons (DPs) were adding to the problem by behaving poorly. At this point, it was likely that all parties preferred to see the GIs return home.

Bob realized the Army needed experienced soldiers to maintain the Constabulary and assist with other military functions. When weighing his opportunities, reenlistment seemed a realistic alternative—especially given the projected increase in the unemployment rate at home.

June 16 1946

Well all the fathers got off safely last night so that is the end of that.

It still has not cleared up yet. Rains every five minutes so that will spoil the whole weekend. I think I told you I do not go swimming but I went down there a couple of times and fooled around but they got me afraid that they will throw me in so I do not go anymore. I do not care for it anyway.

I guess it is just natural that I am afraid of water. One thing is I did not get afraid coming over and enjoyed the trip because I felt at home on a ship. I guess I had been on enough of them.

They are getting the fellows with twenty-one months of service ready to ship home. So that does not leave me with much longer to go. I hope at the latest only another two and a half months. That would bring me home in the first part of September. I can remember when I thought I was coming home last July on the way to the Pacific. They said that some of those fellows got discharged when they got home. But maybe some of them went to

---

the pacific and then I probably wished I was back here.

All I am doing is waiting for time to go by and hoping. I am always thinking that there is still a chance that they will cut it down to eighteen months. I do not know how to describe it but it is an awful wait. Maybe it is like you waiting for something in a line but there you are waiting for something besides time. That's all life is I guess is waiting for something or another. When you are waiting you do not care except when will it come. I do not care if the whole army falls apart. But right now if these people could practically control, the army. And in most cases they are doing it through a favor for somebody. When Gen Harmon first talked to us I thought there is a guy who will get this job done. But when he had talked to us the next time he had calmed down. Maybe somebody had applied the pressure to him.

When I used to deliver the stuff to UNRRA I saw these Pollacks sitting around and then you see piles of empty boxes with a red cross and relief shipper from the United States and a big American flag and these people are not even looking for a way to make a living. And if I was in the same position I would do the same thing. I do not say they are not starving in some parts but god damn let us feed them where they are starving not where they could get along without it.

I have no complaint about our food we are eating good now but why should we not eat the best. We are supposed to be big shots over here representing the American people. But they will never get anyplace with me here because all I do is think of home and so do the rest of the drafted boys. They should get the regular army guy who asked for it.

Bob seemed to become slightly disillusioned with the good works the US Army was doing. What Bob could not have known is that General Harmon had his hands full with recruitment and training of the Constabulary, and he was dealing with the Soviets on a real time basis. Earlier in February 1946, the US Constabulary existed on paper only. By mid-February, Harmon had selected a headquarters staff to implement the plan.

By June, Harmon was also dealing with significant unrest among US soldiers who wanted to go home. It was likely that General Harmon was setting an appropriate tone for the Constabulary to follow at the time, in sharp contrast to General Patton and his aggressive "take all prisoners" tone.

June 17 1946

This is just an after dinner letter it is only a little after one and things are pretty slow I took the afternoon off. The weather is about the same . . . I wish the time would go by faster no matter how fast it goes it is not fast enough. I want to come home in the worst way and yet I am not sure what will happen when I get there. I am just undecided on what to do.

Maybe it is the feeling of getting so close to coming and yet you do not know which way to turn. They say that a big shipment is going out of this outfit the sixteenth of next month.

Wrote about five letters yesterday to everybody including Slim's mother.

It was real quiet yesterday and it rained practically all day. It is pretty quiet all the time now with Slim gone. Now I sleep with the message centre boss and he hangs out with a different crowd. You might call them the big wheels of the outfit. I do not believe that I will ever have the times that Slim and I used to have. If I do I do not know how. I got a good idea that that is what makes the time go so slow. I may not know it but one time you had to have three years to get out. If I do get out at two I guess I will be lucky.

I guess that is all for now and I am going to take a bath.

Love

Bobby Bobby

Mistake HaHaHaHaHaHa

June 17 1946

This is the second letter for today and by the way I did not get any mail tonight. Maybe it is the bad weather at home

It is after eight o'clock and I just got back from a German class. Now that I am getting ready to go home they are trying to teach me that. We have a good time there anyhow. I get all (twisted) up but I can speak it pretty good.

Mom it is in the Stars and Stripes that they are shipping fellows home with twenty one months. It is coming down all the time so one of these days it will come. Might say there is a great day coming.

Every day I do less and less. I stayed home all afternoon and just took it easy. Joe that is the chief says that we will take an afternoon off apiece because these new fellows can handle what work there is and all we do is supervise.

I guess I write the same thing over and over but I have to do something to pass the time.

The cornels wife and two kids are here now. When they first get over they all had the measles but I guess that are all right now. His wife does not look over twenty five. I do not know why anybody would want to bring there family over here. There is nothing to do for them and I don't know but it is beyond me.

Let me explain something. If I do go out and then decide to come back I have to start all over again. That is why I have been thinking. I am between two things and do not know which way to turn. The way it is now I would jump two stripes in a month and be my own boss. It is pretty hard to let go and step out in to insecurity. If I could not get a good job I would come back in. Tell the truth. How is the job situation?

I will sign off now hoping that everything is alright and will stay that way.

LOVE

"BOB"

As part of his Constabulary training, Bob was learning how to speak German. His command of the language disappeared entirely when he returned home.

June 18 1946

Nothing new today no mail again but nobody got any tonight so I guess it is alright.

It has been raining on and off again today. I remember it rained like this last year only we were living in tents. I read about the storm you had at home (in) the paper.

We are going to move for sure this time because they are getting everything packed and the advance party has gone up to Bayreuth. They say we are going to move into barracks up there and that they are all broken down with no windows or anything. It cannot be too bad. Every day counts as it goes by towards coming home.

This month seems to be going by pretty good every days goes is marked off the calendar.

I think I will be glad to get out of this town because I am getting tired of looking at this place. I bet I have been on every street in this town. The change will probably make the time go faster too as it will be new and the time always goes faster when I its something new.

The coronel is going to give a talk tonight so as usual it is on your own time.

I often wonder where I will be a year from now? And never find the answer I guess you never know what is around the corner of the next day.

June 24, 1946

Well you will learn as we proceed with this letter that I have not received any mail. For the last couple of days in Ulm I did not get any. Saturday we got up at three thirty and left at six to come here to Bayreuth and we finally got here at around three and it rained just as hard as possible all the way. I believe it was the most miserable day since I left the infantry.

The living conditions are very poor here. Headquarters troop has about the best billets out of the bunch but we are in a concern where D.P. used to live so you can imagine what the place is like. About one hundred of the boys sent a cablegram to Washington to ask for an I.G. inspection. The doctor has condemned one of the buildings but I do not believe it will do any good.

Monday all the fellows with twenty one months of service as of the end of June are leaving for home so as you can see they are coming down I am coming up with the service. It will not be much longer!

Before I forget I had better tell you my new A.P.O. it is I79. So do not forget to put it on.

I guess we have come to the end of the story for today as I have just about run out of it.

Hope all of you are alright and feeling good and hope to see you soon. Which will probably be quick.

June 25, 1946

Dear Dad,

Well here we go on another excursion and we shall see what will come of it. The latest thing is that they are going to move most of the squadron out in tents because of all the complaints. Some of the fellows think that it will be better than staying in this place. Maybe it will and then again maybe it will not.

I do not think it will be much longer for me as they are getting nearer me all the time with this redeployment. They are coming down all the time and have finally reached twenty one months and I will have nineteen at the end of this month. And I think that is getting close. Close enough to hope anyway.

I think I lost my best friend I ever had when Slim went home. Since then I have lost Whitey is in the hospital with an infected finger or I should say hand. I went up to see him today and they had it all bandaged up and now he has a boil on his rear end and they cut that open. So he is in pretty bad shape but even at that we still got a coke. I will go see him again tomorrow and take him some cigarettes. He is a good egg but a little too wild for me to go around with. When he goes any place he always gets into some kind of trouble. The only reason that he and I are such good friends is that he come in the army the same day and have gone the same places ever since.

This town we are in now is pretty small besides Ulm but it has got good recreational facilities. It has got a big red cross and a couple of good clubs and a large movies. So that is what makes it good.

Well I think that is about all for now and will sign off.

Do not forget to answer this letter.

LOVE

BOB

June 25 1946

. . . the mailman went to Stuggart today to get the mail so I guess tomorrow or the next day I ought to get some mail. I can hope cant I?

Do not forget to put the new A.P.O. on or it will still go to the old place and I could use a little morale builder.

The time is drawing near when old Glover will be back on the sidewalks of old New York.

They just got me on C.Q. by surprise so maybe this letter will be longer than I thought . . .

This is a different typewriter than I had before as you have probably noticed and I cannot get it adjusted so it makes no difference.

Some days I am all for staying in this army then the next day I am all against it so as you will realize as time goes by that I cannot make up my mind what to do. I think I will come home. I have come to that conclusion since we moved to this place. It is a mess here.

Whitey is in the hospital with an infected hand. I have not seen him since but it looked pretty bad when he left. I think I will get a chance to see him this afternoon.

Slim ought to be in the states by this time I think.

I honestly think I will be home this summer. Things look good over here. According to my figures I ought to leave this outfit sometime in July and everybody else has the same idea.

I only hope that they are guessing right. When my time comes I am going to be finished for good. I hope.

How is everybody and everything at home?

Well the sun is trying to get out, if it does it will be a miracle. That word is hard to spell. I do not know (why) I always put three l s for I guess I get excited.

I guess that is about all at this time.

Well it is six o'clock and I am back on cq again. When you are on cq you pull from twelve to one and from five thirty in the afternoon till eight in the morning. It is not too bad but it gets tiresome.

Everybody is running around wild here, a couple of water pipes broke and now the c.o. and all his boys are running around like mad. What a hole we are in. I will be glad to get out.

The boys are complaining all over but it does not seem to do any good. The trouble is the officers are living in some hotel and the others are living in private homes. If they had to live here things would be different. I do not think it told you all the trouble we have encountered here, first in most of the places there are no lights, most of the toilets are clogged, the places stink, all of it is real dirty, the yards are full of trash, half the windows are out and then they wonder why the fellows complain.

The fellows ought to get some kind of action as they have wrote to the commanding general of the constabulary and cabled to the surgeon general at Washington.

One of these days I am going to send you a telegram so do not get excited if you get one.

I guess that is all for today and excuse the errors.

June 27 1946

Well seeing that they got back from Stuttgart with the mail I received three letters and a package. Two letters for you and one from Butch. It sure does make a fellow feel better when you get some mail. Now I shall try to answer . . .

I guess they kid Felix about swimming like they do me but it does not bother me very much. I went down there a couple of times but I could never swim and never be able to.

Maybe this pass that Carl is getting will wind up his stay in the States.

We received some letters from fellows who got discharged and they say you feel lost when you get out and feel like joining again. I know darn well I will feel that way because there is nobody that I know to pal around with and I guess that after a while a fellow gets lonesome and takes the wrong road again. I just hope that does not happen to me.

You said that you thought Slim was home well I guess he ought to be by now. One of these days when I get home I am going to take that trip to Louisville Kentucky and see him. I tried to get him to come to New York but he said that he would never so I shall go and see him.

I have just answered the letter of the eighteenth so now we go to the nineteenth. This is a shorter letter than the other one.

Do what you please with the camera I have no more use for it and I still have Dolly's. I think I will wait till I come home to bring the other one. It cost forty two bucks and I think I can keep it safe till I get there.

Yes it does look as if I might get out one of these days in the not too distant future. I hope that it comes quicker than I think.

What do you mean that things do not look as though they will ever be settled again? Is Daddy working? If so what is he doing? Tell me these things it is something to write about. If it is not asking too much will you write and tell me how much money I have in the bank and otherwise.

Is it enough to amount to anything or not?

Sorry to hear that you have not been feeling good.

Well I guess that is all for now and will write again when there is something to write about.

Sunday June 30 1946

It is Sunday so I went to see Whitey at the hospital again. His hand is getting along good so I think he will get out in a week or so.

I have some great news but I don't want you to get all excited and then something go wrong. I am suppose to leave from here and start on my way home the twentieth of July. I have been disappointed so many times that I am not to excited. But they claim it is the truth. Wed. the third of July the men with twenty one leave then the tenth those with twenty leave and the twentieth the fellows with nineteen are suppose to start. It will be on or about that date so that is all you can say on that subject. We shall forget about it and you write just the same the only thing is do not send any more packages. If everything goes according to schedule I should be home for good in the first or second week of August.

It has been plenty hot these last couple of days, just sweat all the time.

I hope that I will get a job and get along good at it that is the only thing that worries me. When I was eating dinner today I happened to think that you said Carl would be home the first of July and I felt pretty lousey. I think I was made to be a home boy I never did go anyplace much and I am still that way and I think I always will be.

I think that is about all as I have not received any mail except those letters they got when they went to Stuttgart.

JULY 1946—PLASTICS

July 1 1946

Well here I go again . . .

There is nothing further on that coming home business, all we can do is hope that I get home before winter. I do not believe that time has ever gone so slow before. As I have told you before that the way I look at it that you spend most of your life waiting for something and then you start to wait for something else.

First I was waiting to get in the army then you wait to finish your basic then you wait to go overseas then you start to wait to go home.

I think that is what makes a fellow stay in the army so long is that you are always waiting. But I bet that wait from now till I get home will be the longest wait that I ever had.

What else is there to say in a letter? I try to write something to you and you probably get all mad because well I write so you get a letter not because I have something to write. What to write about next has got me stumped.

I could write about the weather except it is about the same all the time and for the last couple of days it has been real warm that ends that and now is my time to strain my brain (if any) and try to think of something else to write.

Oh yes while I think of it if you happen to go by the army navy store on 181 street you can get me some ribbons for me if you will get the kind that is hooked together I want three in a one set when you have it on will be from left to right E.T.O. victory and occupation and do not worry about that good conduct as I can get plenty of them. Send them air mail to me if you will.

Now in to another coma and try and think that I am home and somebody is writing to me and see what would they say.

I guess that I have told you a couple of times that I would like to go to Kentucky and see Slim sometime if I ever get a chance. What do you think? Do you think I will ever get around to it?

That is about the only place that I want to proceed to when I hit that old New York.

I hear that there is a good plastic school in Rochester so maybe if the navy yard does not come through that I will take a swing at that. Let me know what you think about some of these crazy ideas that I get. Do you think that I could afford it or do you think that I should keep after the sheet metal? You have not given me very much advice since I have been over here. Do not think that I am too old yet to take some advice. It always helps anybody. Where will I be in a year and what will I be doing that is the big question.

I know darn well that I do not want an office job I want some other kind of work

What are some of the other guys doing around the old street you must hear what the fellows are doing are most of them just collecting the twenty dollars a week and taking it easy or are they working. I know darn well that they are not giving the guys to big of a break because these guys come over and say they are getting a raw deal, and I guess they are.

Well I think that's that for today and hope that I get some mail tonight

---

July 4 1946

Dear dad,

I will try to write you a letter but it will probably be short as there is very little to write about.

I told the boys you were making two ten an hour and they were all glad to hear it as I told them you had lost your job in the yard

266

and then you said you had a job but would not say what it was. Then the fellows started to kid me about you being a night watchman. I was sweating out what you were doing myself. Sometime that you have nothing to do write and tell me what they expect you to know in a sheet metal job like that where they are paying so good. I know that all it is is common sense but do you have to do your own layouts or does somebody else do it for you? I know darn well that I could do just as good as some of those first class mechanics in the yard. Do not forget to let me know as I am coming home in the very near future.

Yes sir Dad I will be home in the first part of next month and I have forgot all about staying in the army. I think that I have had my share of it.

Why do you not get after Mom and try to get her to see a doctor and see if she cannot get on a diet or something.

Slim was in the states twenty one days after he left this outfit.

I am suppose to leave the twentieth of this month so that I am feeling happy and have quit doing any work and just loaf around and take it easy.

Yesterday I went to Nuremberg to take some stuff but I went because I had never been there.

Boy it has been so hot the last week that you just sweat like a pig all the time, and now they have developed a water shortage.

Tomorrow the Life magazine is going to take a picture of the regiment so I will have my picture in a magazine but you will never tell whether it is me or somebody else.

Well I think that is all for now and I expect an answer from you in the near future.

Bob was trying to reintegrate himself into the family by discussing his mother's personal issues, and for many years,

Louise had been on the heavy side—however, that was hardly wise subject for Bob to comment upon, no matter how homesick he was. Roy was patient with Bob, but likely considered Bob to have crossed the line here.

July 6 1946

I did not receive any mail in the last couple of days. I hope that you are not expecting me home already and have quit writing.

The fellows with twenty one months of service left this morning, so that is one step nearer for me.

It finally rained last night after two weeks of very hot weather so now it is a little cooler.

There has been no change in the date when I am expected to leave.

But they are liable to change the whole thing at the last moment so I just go along hoping that nothing happens to change it.

Well I get more impatient every day that is I think more and more about getting out.

Yesterday the Life photographer took our picture but we left the barracks here at eight in the morning and got back at three. We were out on an open field all that time and the sun was never so hot before. The guy that took the picture was some DP or something and he did not seem to care how long we stood there. Finally he took some from the air and it was over.

If that fellow was ever cussed he was cussed yesterday. If they do put the picture in the magazine you look for a fellow in the very last row with his helmet liner off and that is me. What they will go through for a picture.

Cigarettes are very hard to sell in this town and now I am about forty dollars on my currency control book. The reason that they

---

> *are so hard to sell is that they have got a lot of C.I.C. men in this town and nobody wants to take a chance. They caught one fellow and he got six months out of it.*

The Counter Intelligence Corps (CIC) was assigned to preventing US soldiers from trading on the black market. Soldiers who had made an easy profit a few months ago selling cigarettes and watches were now on guard. The Army began to enforce the rules; if a soldier were caught trading, he would be punished.

July 8 1946

. . .

Wrote a letter to Slim this morning but I find the same trouble trying to write to him as I do to you . . .

They have postponed the fellows who were to leave this Wednesday till next Monday so that will set me back a week or so. I hope that you had not got your hopes up high when I told you around the twentieth as I told you they would probably change it. They want to keep you on edge until you get out. I think the best thing to do would be to forget about it but that is pretty hard to do.

The mail situation has been bad for the last couple of weeks it seems that I write about three times as many letters as I get.

Daddy said that you were not feeling good maybe that is the reason you do not write so much. Why don't you see a doctor and see if he cannot help you as there must be something that you are able to do. I think myself that you are too big maybe if you got rid of some of that fat you would feel better. Well you know what you want to do so that is all that I can say.

Well I think now is a good time to start to talk about jobs.

Some body is lieing as the fellows say that you cannot get a job then you say that there is plenty of jobs. Are you just trying to get me to come home or is there work? No use kidding me because I have decided to come home at any cost. They way that I have felt since we moved to this town I would not stay in this for love or money. I think with this new raise that I will get about hundred and fifteen a month but that is still not for me. I have hundred and fifty on the book now and only have about hundred and I have to get P.X. rations this afternoon and that will some off my book as anything over fifty cents comes off now.

I am not doing a darn thing now all I do is sit in this place and put the time in. Wrote a letter to Slim this morning and that is all I did.

I also got a half a day of work for missing revile this morning.

The first sergeant asked me if I wanted that or the one hundred and four so I took the half of day.

How is Janet and the rest of the tribe?

They say that when you leave here you go to Nuremburg then the next day go by train to the port.

I never thought that Bud would be married as I don't know but it does not sound right but I think that he was twenty when I first met him!

Who the heck will I know that I can fool around with when I get home?

If I get too lonely I will have to go down and see Slim.

Don't forget to let me know what is going on in that Bronx at that job and how Dad is making out. I am kind of interested in how he gets along.

Did Carl ever get home on furlough yet or is he going to another school? I think that (he) is plenty lucky to stay in the states so long.

Every day seems to go slower and slower for me as I get nearer to that last mile. But from the news today that these fellows are not leaving for another five days it looks as if I will get home sometime in the winter.

Well I guess that Joanie is getting up in the world now that she has finished high school.

I cannot understand what Dolly is taking up this steno typing for.

July 10 1946

Seeing that I did not write to you yesterday . . .

You said that I should have told Slim to stop in and see you.

Well I told him if he had any extra time to see you but he did not think much of New York. Maybe when I get home I will get him to come up for a week or so. As I told you before I am going to see him sometime when I get some time.

Every day is dragging and it seems that it will never pass. The shipment that was going to leave today was postponed until Monday. So you can see that I will be lucky to get out of here this month.

I do not remember what pictures that was that I sent home and you say they were so good.

Your letter came in seven days . . .

I seen that picture The Road to Utopia.

Last night I seen a USO show at the red cross the name of it was touch and go well they could keep right on going because it was not so hot.

When I find out definitely what day I am leaving this outfit I will try to send you a cablegram so if you do happen to get one do not get all excited.

I was thinking the other night as I was trying to go to sleep that some time it would be nice to go crabbing again. I think that it was always a lot of fun.

Nowadays I can seem to go to sleep at any time of the day. Maybe it is the weather and maybe it is that I could use some exercise

They took a second Lt. away to the hospital this morning as he was going to Stuttgart with Superman and having imaginary fights with the colonel's wife. He had just lost his head completely. I never did think that he was any good and I think they will have another one in a couple of days . . .

I often wonder what I will be doing next year at this time and different things like that. When I think to myself that I will be twenty this month I feel kind of old. I do not think I should feel this way. When I come into this army I never thought I would get out so quick and some ho sometimes I do not feel I am ready to come home.

July 19 1946 . . .

I received the birthday cards they were all very nice.

Nothing has been said about leaving here Monday so I guess that we will have to keep on waiting. It has got to be sometime next week as they say over the radio that the nineteen month fellows are starting to come into Bremerhaven already but this Constabulary is a couple of weeks behind the other outfit so it has got to be next week as I am going crazy waiting.

We all expected to go Monday as that is the way they have been spacing the shipments, now that there is nothing on Monday the strain of waiting is getting worse. I think that once I start on my way I will feel a heck of a lot better. Right now that is all that I have on my mind.

Your letters come in four days they are getting better all the time.

I do not know if I told you or not but I got another camera. This is an I20 got distance and some other stuff like that, it cost $12 in the P.X. so it must be a better one than the one I sent home.

I have not had any luck getting a watch or harmonica for Doll but I will keep trying.

Mom one minute you hear that you are going home Monday then the next it is just a rumor.

I will send you a cable gram when I find out for sure when I am leaving. Do not get all excited if you receive one.

July 23 1946

Well here it is Tuesday already and there is still nothing about coming home. It seems that every time that I am ready to do something like that something always goes wrong. But I do not think it will be too much longer as the fellows in Berlin have already started so it will be sometime this week. I hope. They said that they did not have enough ships so they had to postpone us for a week. They will have to start us pretty soon or else I will have twenty months.

There is very little to write about . . .

I just wrote this so that you would get mail and that is all there is to write about.

July 24 1946

Well there was no mail again today but I guess you think I will be home pretty soon and I hope that you are thinking right because now we are suppose to leave here the last day of the month. And they say that is for sure. I hope that this is the last time they change it as I have got so discussed that it does not matter anymore.

If I do catch this one I will be lucky because Whitey come in the army on the second of the month and I come in the first and that just put me over, that is nineteen month as of the end of June. Whitey has missed by one day. There are a couple of fellows like that who just missed it because they come in on the second. . . . Well what is done is done so we shall just have to leave Whitey here.

I will send you a cablegram when I find out for sure

I think that I will have a little money when I get out as I have one and a half hundred and then I will have this months pay coming and some of next months and some of that other stuff they throw in.

July 25 1946

Well another day has gone by and the time is drawing near when I will get home. There was no mail again yesterday as you have probably quit writing.

The days are going along but they are going pretty slow. I suppose that they will fly be when I get home. How is Dad doing and the rest of the gang. I am undecided what to do when I get home as that money sounds awful good and the navy yard could never compare with those wages.

I think that if I can get a good high paying job that it would be best to take it as there will be a slump or depression or something as after every war it is bound to come all that anybody can do is to prolong it.

Yes, I think that the navy yard will wait or they can dump the whole thing.

Maybe I could get a job there anyway. What would probably

happen is that I would go work there for a year or so and then they would say that they were sorry but did not have any work. When I get home I will take a ride over to Brooklyn and see what they say. I think that I was getting seventy cents an hour there and I know that I will not work for that.

We shall see what will happen and then we will decide. I think that I will take a vacation and look the city over a bit and maybe take a little trip some place

Well I guess that is all for today.

Am suppose to leave the thirty first of this month.

July 26 1946

Well another day has passed and that brings me one day closer to getting out. There is only four more days left in this outfit so I will probably be on my way before I know it. The days are going by pretty good now and I hope they keep going that way. The next thing that I have to sweat out is the wait at the port which will be Bremerhaven. They say you are there five days to a week so that will be another wait. No mail again yesterday . . .

We are having hot weather here in fact it is too hot most of the time.

Whitey cracked up a jeep last night so he will probably get into some more trouble as he was not suppose to be out with it. It seems that he is always in trouble.

I got two camera cases last night one for the camera you sent and the other for the other camera. They are not made out of such good stuff but they will do to get them home in.

I have been coming home so long and never got there I hope I make it this time.

Will I ever get enough sleep it seems that all I want to do is sleep and I can go to sleep at any time without any trouble. I can sleep sixteen hours and then get up and want more sleep . . .

July 27 1946

Well last night I finally received a letter from you but I had forgotten that you had went to Greenport. It was good to hear from you again as it had been quite a while and I thought you had quit writing already.

Well far as we know we are still suppose to leave here next Monday.

We hear over the radio that the eighteen month fellows are starting to come in and we are still here with nineteen. Some of this stuff that you hear is very discouraging and then you think you will be on your way in a couple of days and then it is not so bad. It seems that the time will never go by sometimes and then you forget about it for a while then another days has passed. I have three and a half more nights here and three days.

I will try to tell you how we go well we leave here at three thirty Wednesday and go to Nuremburg and there we catch the seven o'clock train and we ride for a day and a half and should get to Bremerhaven Thursday afternoon if everything goes alright. Then you have to get processed there and then you start to wait again that wait is indefinite all you can do is hope that you hit it when the place is clear of men and the ships are on schedule if they are it will only be about four days there if not you will probably be there a week or a little more. Let's hope that everything is on time or ahead of time. I will probably hit it and have to stay there three weeks as that is the kind of luck I have.

What is so bad as waiting for the ship to come in another thing is that they did not waste any time getting me over here I was only in Camp Shanks for twenty three hours and they had the boat

> *waiting for me.*
>
> *Well I think that is all for today as I have run out of stuff to write about and that is enough for today.*

No letter was found in the box dated July 28th. Hopefully Bob was busy celebrating his twentieth birthday.

> *July 29 1946*
>
> *Well there is nothing new and I am just writing so that you know I am still around and still waiting. As far as I know we are going to leave the thirty first and that is only a couple more days.*
>
> *As you know yesterday was my birthday and I didn't realize it until it was about seven o'clock and Whitey and I were at the club and Whitey got the orchestra to play and sing it so it was not too bad. Then he got sad and started to cry because he was not going home with me, altogether it was quite an evening. I will not forget it for a long time and that is for sure. Whitey is a good hearted egg but is also too crazy.*
>
> *I have turned in all the stuff that I am not going to take with me and I am ready to pack all that I have to do is throw the stuff in the bag and take off.*
>
> *Figure that you get this letter in a week will by then I hope to be on the boat. I only hope that I am. I hope to be finished with this army by the fifteenth of August.*
>
> *That is all there is to say I mean that is all there is to say.*

Bob's closing sentence in his final letter was likely inspired by a quote from General G. S. Patton: "Say what you mean and mean what you say."

EPILOGUE

At the end of July 1946, and for the first time since March/April 1945, the steady stream of letters ceased. Bob had finally received his orders and was on his way home.

Bob's unit had moved several times since his arrival in Germany, from Wickrathberg to Mönchengladbach to Heidelberg and to Weither. During the last few months, he was stationed in Hall and Ulm.

Following the end of the war, Bob's responsibilities as a Reconnaissance Scout, and Jeep driver for the Message Center enabled him to travel from city to city on a routine basis and observe the aftereffects of the war. He saw firsthand the results of many of the events that have since been described in books, movies, and other media about World War II. Upon his return to civilian life he, like many veterans, did not speak often about his experiences. Though he took many graphic photos, he never mentioned the details of concentration camps or POW camps in his letters. Or if he had, any references to the horrors he witnessed would likely have been redacted/edited as part of the V-mail censor system.

Bob's letters stopped because Bob was moving west across Europe and eventually across the Atlantic Ocean. He departed from Europe on August 8, 1946, and disembarked in the United States on August 25, 1946. The trip from Germany to the United States took a full seventeen days.

On August 30th, Bob was awarded an Honorable Discharge from the Army, with his rank noted as: Technician, Fourth Grade. Per Army policy, detailed records were kept of Bob's time served inside the US and outside; he was credited with four months and twenty days of "Continental" service and one year, four months, and ten days of "Foreign" service.

According to Army records, primarily for compensation purposes, he had served a total of one year, nine months, and zero days. His "mustering out pay" was three hundred dollars.

His life insurance policy was scheduled to be discontinued at the end of August, unless he chose to pay a monthly premium of $6.40. Bob did not renew the policy and, as later in life, chose to put the money to better use and invest it in other opportunities.

His last official Army organization was listed as Headquarters Company, 13th Tank Battalion, and his separation date from the Army was August 30, 1946 at Fort Dix in New Jersey. His military history was recorded, and his final title was listed as an occupational specialty, Message Center Clerk.

He was credited with being in the Battle of Northern France and received the Army of the Occupation medal, the European African, Middle Eastern Campaign medal, and the World War II Victory Medal. The Army credited him as having several immunizations but no wounds received in action.

Bob was fortunate to have served under good leaders for much of his time in the Army; he drove two notable Silver Star award officers for periods of time in his Jeep: Lt. Donald H. Dearborn, and Lt. Richard Swope.

Bob decided to list his civilian occupation as a sheet metal worker.

On the afternoon of the day Bob was discharged, Butch, now 9 years old, was across the street from his apartment building at a friend's home. It was a hot, sunny day and the two boys were playing on the fire escape landing outside the second floor apartment window when they saw a taxi stop in front of Butch's apartment building. Butch watched as the rear door of the cab popped open and a fully packed, army green duffle bag appeared. The bag was followed by a young soldier in uniform. Without saying goodbye to his friend, Butch rushed through the apartment building, down the stairs and across the street to his family's apartment. He was thrilled to confirm what he suspected, he had watched his big brother Bob exit the cab; he had finally arrived home.

∞∞ ∞∞ ∞∞

In 1946, Bob re-entered the civilian world, like millions of his wartime buddies.

Postwar jobs were difficult to find in the New York metropolitan area; however, there were plenty of educational and job training opportunities available with some funding, and Bob chose eventually to work for the city of New York. In 1951, he entered the New York City Police Department and put some, if not all, of his Army Constabulary training to good use. He was assigned for the most part in the 30th Precinct (Harlem area) and the 34th Precinct (Washington Heights area, near the George Washington Bridge).

As a police recruit, Bob lived with his parents in their apartment and spent long hours learning how to perform many of the tasks required of an officer of the law, including apprehension of suspected criminals.

Early in his police career, Bob got the opportunity to put his new skills to work. His father, Roy, often made friends among his new colleagues. One night, Roy invited one of these new friends to dinner at his home; however, shortly after the invitation was extended, Roy learned he had to work overtime. Roy handed his key to his new friend and gave him directions to the Glovers' apartment, knowing that his wife Louise was with her relatives in Long Island and wouldn't be bothered if his coworker waited inside for Roy to get home.

Encouraged by Roy's generosity, the friend accepted the offer and headed to the apartment in Washington Heights. After knocking several times, he unlocked the door and let himself in. Feeling tired after a full day's work, he went into the bedroom to take a nap, knowing that Roy would wake him when he arrived.

Outside the apartment, the old elevator groaned its arrival outside the apartment door and Louise, who was no longer on Long Island, stepped into the hallway. She readjusted her shopping bags to find her key, unlocked the door, and entered the apartment. She made her way to the kitchen to unload the bags, and afterward went to change her clothes in the bedroom. Upon entering, she sensed there was something unusual about the room and screamed when she saw a strange man sleeping atop her bed. The invited guest—woken from a deep sleep—was groggy and had no idea who this woman was and why she was yelling at him. It took him a few seconds to come to his senses, but he realized that this screaming woman must be Louise, Roy's wife, come home early!

As he tried to calm her down and explain, the elevator delivered another passenger outside the Glover apartment door. If it had been Roy, the situation would have been quickly resolved.

Unfortunately for the guest, it was Bob, now an NYPD officer and a trained WWII ex-combat soldier, just getting off his work shift. He heard his mother's screams and he rushed into the apartment, using his combat training and new police skills to apprehend the intruder, threatening that the stranger had made a serious mistake entering the apartment.

The guest pleaded to explain and edged his way to the door. Bob backed him out the front door, and just then the elevator door opened again. Roy stepped out, holding a new box of cigars and an unopened bottle of whiskey. The would-be guest flew past the stunned Roy and disappeared down the stairs, never to see the apartment again.

It is unknown if Roy was ever able to explain or apologize to his friend, but he certainly had a good story to tell while enjoying his cigars and whiskey.

AUTHOR'S EPILOGUE

The rest of the story of the letter box relates to the hopes and dreams of my father, many of which he was able to make happen.

He was introduced by mutual friends to his future wife—my mother—Joan, and they married in 1952. By 1957 they had three children; in 1953, Joseph was born, I was born in 1954, and finally Robert Jr. was born in 1957. We lived in an apartment in Washington Heights, a few blocks from Roy and Louise. However, in 1960, they decided we needed a larger place to live, so we moved from our apartment to a new house in Nanuet, NY.

Dad commuted to his police job in Manhattan for many years; the route occasionally took him past Camp Shanks, now a suburban community to his precincts in Upper Manhattan. In 1966, he was promoted to the rank of sergeant. He had several tough assignments, and many were undercover roles for which he had to work the night shift from midnight to 8 a.m. The boroughs of New York City during the seventies and eighties were often dangerous and crime rates grew as the city population grew. There were 2228 murders in NYC in 1980, more than double the rate in 1965. Prostitution and drug trafficking grew significantly as well. Being a cop was a risky job; in 1980, eleven NYPD officers were killed in the line of duty.

Mom became increasingly uncomfortable with the dangers my father faced at work; the daily cuts, scrapes, and bruises were evidence of the challenges of the job. She finally convinced him to retire and take a less risky position.

My parents valued education, and it was a priority for the family. Bob and Joan each received job-related training; my mother had trained at the local pharmaceutical company, where she worked for many years. Looking back, their investment in their children seems to have worked out well; at the time of writing, Joe is Provost of one of the largest public universities in the United States; I have been CEO of several public and private companies; and Rob has been the president of one of the largest unions in the country.

After his police career, our father seemed to enjoy entrepreneurial activities; he had excellent interpersonal skills and worked well with many types of people. After retiring from the NYPD, he explored a variety of positions, including limousine and taxi driving, but the jobs he enjoyed most seemed to be related to food or people.

In what we initially thought was a strange twist for him, Bob leased an ice cream truck during springs, summers, and falls, and sold ice cream in areas such as Spring Valley, Nanuet, and West Nyack. He loved the kids and they had fun with him. He was quick on his feet; once when a young customer asked him "Mr. G, if red ice is cherry flavored and yellow ice is lemon flavored, then (pointing to a picture of a new color of ice) what flavor is this?" Without hesitation, and in his staccato style, our dad simply replied, "Why, that new flavor is called *Blue!*" The boy was thrilled. Several months later the ice cream manufacturer started calling the flavor "raspberry," but for my dad's customers, the flavor was always just "Blue."

Bob also worked in a cheese business that was owned by a friend; the friend made a small fortune in the manufacture and sale of mozzarella-based cheeses. This was a perfect situation for Dad. During the early stages of his employment, he was responsible for driving the owner to cheese shops all over the New York area, selling cheese, and collecting money. When he suggested to the owner that he could do more, the owner put him in charge of smoked cheese production—a perfect job involving food, people, and one of his favorite pastimes: smoking.

He was good at predicting issues of social concern. As an example, well before tobacco became a popular hot-button topic issue in the media and the courtrooms, he forecasted that politicians would eventually prohibit tobacco use in public and eventually "outlaw tobacco." His prediction wasn't too far off the mark.

Dad enjoyed gambling, both Las Vegas-casino style and stock market trading on Wall Street. He got pretty good at both. He and my mother would often travel to the casinos in Vegas or Atlantic City to try their luck at blackjack, slots, and roulette games.

More than a simple hobby, he became very active in trading stocks, and he invested in anything that caught his attention, from blue chips to NASDAQ/OTC. He read everything he could about the market and subscribed to several stock market publications.

However, there was something about his dreams and his experience in Europe that kept him from wanting to return. Occasionally, my mother would bring up the subject of traveling to Europe and would ask to vacation there. Dad always shot that idea down; he wasn't averse to travel—after all, they had taken long trips to Las Vegas, California, and Hawaii—but there was something about returning to Europe that was uncomfortable for him. Once, when driving my older brother to Cornell University in upstate New York, he pointed to the mountains and the trees and remarked, "Why would anyone want to travel to Germany when you can see the same beauty, or more, right in your own backyard?"

On the other hand, several of Dad's family members have been attracted to Europe. Trips involving education (both of his grandchildren studied abroad in places like London and Seville), business and tourism were the key reasons. Though he understood the need for others to travel there, he himself preferred to visit other places.

During the war, my father and millions of other soldiers enriched millions of current and future lives by preserving the free world and the opportunities that go along with that concept. For instance, his granddaughter—my daughter—Katie lived in England as a student and interned at one of the most prestigious art museums in the world. During that time, she was able to tour the Churchill Cabinet War Rooms on Charles Street in London, a secret underground headquarters for Churchill and his staff during World War II. The time Katie spent there enriched her life and provided memories that would not be possible without her grandfather's and his buddies' role in the war.

One place Dad did return to on occasion was his boyhood home in Cutchogue; no matter how much time passed, the lure of the North Fork remained strong.

Dad's army friends and their whereabouts, unfortunately, have been lost to us. Over the years, Dad and Whitey talked a few times by phone—mostly to reminisce about the good times in Europe. Like many WWII veterans, there was little discussion about any bad times. They shared a story about "borrowing" a train one night and driving it several miles, in reverse, so they could get fresh donuts at the Red Cross. They often asked each other if they had they seen "any old buddies?" But the answer was always the same: no, they hadn't. Life had gotten in the way.

But who knows? Whitey had a habit of disappearing for long periods of time; maybe he will pop up again.

After the war's end, Slim moved back home to Kentucky. On a road trip a few years ago, my younger brother, Rob, and his wife, Terri, visited Slim and had lunch together. Slim had very fond memories of the unit and our father. Rob reported that Slim was still as solemn as Dad had mentioned in his letters from 1945, and he shared very little about their war-related experiences.

Two of his New York/New Jersey area friends, Pvt. E. A. Guadagno and Art Sarno have also been lost to history.

However, on special occasions and holidays, our family would visit with Dad's sisters and brother and their families.

After living in northern Manhattan for many years, Uncle Rich "Butch" and his wife, Erna, moved to Sloatsburg, NY, and they have two wonderful children and several grandchildren.

Janet married Charlie Smith and moved to southern California, a wonderful place to be for their three children and lots of grandchildren and great-grandchildren.

Dolly married Carl and had two children, but after a few years of marriage, they divorced. Dad would have said, "No comment. Let it go."

True "salts of the earth," Louise and Roy were very fortunate; they had several children and grandchildren who cared for them deeply.

∞∞ ∞∞ ∞∞

The objective of writing this story was to preserve for future generations the comments and experiences of one young soldier during his time in World War II.

Many of the places that Dad knew best as a soldier in Europe would likely be unrecognizable today. Europe, thankfully, has rebuilt most of the cities destroyed during the war. However, some scars still remain.

Bob's World War II "keepsakes" will continue to be preserved for many to learn from in the years to come. Their value is worth much more than Dad could ever have predicted. His war photos were donated to the University of Florida, and his pistol was donated to the military museum at West Point.

Dad passed away in 1998. His service in the United States Army was not forgotten—a military honor guard presided over his funeral.

His army jacket continues to hang in a Glover family closet.

No one is quite sure where Butch's helmet is.

And the letters? Oh, the letters. They are in the box, also in a Glover family closet. Still! For future generations and inquisitive minds, who want to know what Grandpa Bob did in World War II.

Thanks, Dad, for taking the time to write these letters.

PHOTOGRAPHS AND A MAP

Private Robert Glover, US Army—1945

Map of Central Europe—1945

Examples of Two Letters

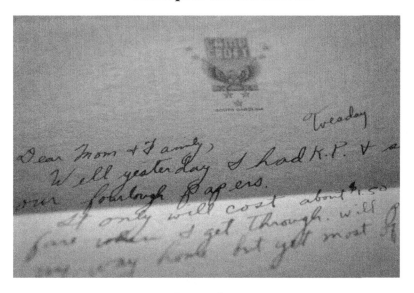

December 1944

January 1945

Pvt. Bob Glover, "Somewhere in Germany, 1945"

In addition to the letters, bank notes were sometimes enclosed, like this Belgian Frank.

Janet, "Dolly" (Ruth), "Butch" (Rich), and Bob. NYC

Bob's ODs (Olive Drabs)

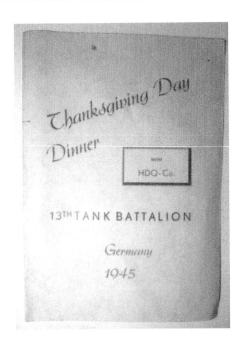

Thanksgiving Day Menu. November 1945

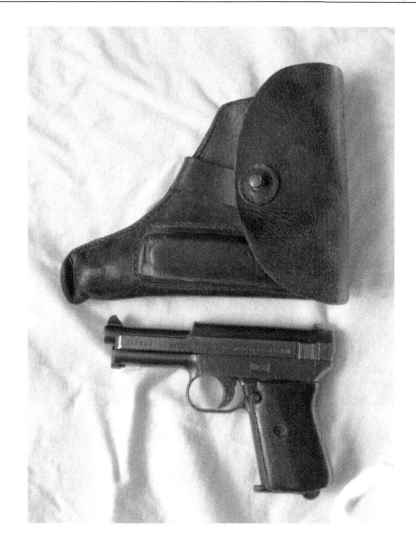

The .32 Mauser pistol. Now in the West Point Museum

Louise and Roy Glover, with grandson Joseph Glover, 1953

Bob Glover and family, 1966

Made in the USA
Middletown, DE
09 January 2023

21146111R00176